COME RAIN
COME SHINE

24⁸

COME RAIN COME SHINE

JOHN MOORE

ALAN SUTTON
1983

Alan Sutton Publishing Limited
17a Brunswick Road
Gloucester GL1 1HG

Copyright © 1956 John Moore

First published 1956 by Collins
This edition published 1983

ISBN 0-86299-103-X

Cover picture: detail from Golding Constable's Flower Garden *by John Constable.*
Ipswich Borough Council

Printed and bound in Great Britain
by Redwood Burn Limited, Trowbridge

Acknowledgements

My thanks are due to the authors and publishers for permission to use extracts and quotations from the following works: *I Had a Dog and A Cat* by Karel Capek (Allen & Unwin Ltd.), *The Spider* by John Crompton (Collins), *Collected Poems* by Walter de la Mare (Faber & Faber Ltd.), *Family Reunion* by Ogden Nash (J. M. Dent & Sons Ltd.), *Birds of A Valley* by W. R. Philipson (Longmans Green & Co. Ltd.), *The Walls of Glass* by A. S. J. Tessimond (Methuen & Co. Ltd.); to the authors' executors and to the publishers for permission to use extracts and quotations from the following: *The Shropshire Lad* by A. E. Housman (Jonathan Cape Ltd.), *Rewards and Fairies* by Rudyard Kipling (Macmillan & Co. Ltd. and the Macmillan Co. of Canada), *Book of a Naturalist* by W. H. Hudson (J. M. Dent & Sons Ltd.), *Collected Poems* by Edward Thomas (Faber & Faber Ltd.), *Collected Poems* by Dylan Thomas (J. M. Dent & Sons Ltd.), and to Mrs. Wild for permission to quote from the note books of the late Dr. Oliver H. Wild. Like *The Season of the Year*, to which this is a companion volume, this book has grown out of occasional writings which in a different form were printed or broadcast; so I should like to add my acknowledgements to the B.B.C., the *Observer*, *The Saturday Book* and the *Birmingham Mail*.

CONTENTS

Part One

THE BACKEND OF
THE YEAR

I

WELL, THEY have harvested the oats which were so loud when the wind blew through them, and the barley that whispered as softly as lovers whisper, and the wheat which made only a little dry grasshopper sound. For a short while the stubbles will lie undisturbed, and the sunsets will turn them rust-red, as if the last of the summer's heat smouldered away there. Then the tractors will crawl into them, and the bright ploughshares will turn over the stubbles, and quite suddenly the light will go out of the land, as we enter upon what an old backbent and whisky-pickled Colonel I knew long ago used to call the arse-end of the year.

He loved this arse-end, or backend if you prefer it, the season between autumn ploughing and Christmas, because it spelt for him partridges and pheasants, and the pike which he caught in the Avon, and the eels for which he set wicker traps called putcheons, and the great winds of the equinox, which brought the wild duck and the high geese honking as they flew south. Also he maintained, quite rightly, that the backend was really the beginning of the country year; New Year's Day, if he'd been allowed to arrange it, would have been fixed upon a date round about the time when he planted his winter wheat. Of course in farming operations there is really no end and no beginning, they are like the merry-go-round at our October Fair, when as you stand at Elmbury Cross and look up at the riders on the horses you see the same faces recurring like the seasons, a pretty young girl's face welcome as April, a drunken old fool like November, a blown blowsy woman like July. But if one is going to choose an arbitrary point for beginning a book about country contentments, then the time of the autumn planting is the apt and obvious one. So I begin my book at the backend; and because the old Colonel's autumnal face is in my mind as I start writing, let me introduce him now.

EVERY MORNING at precisely five to twelve, and every evening on the stroke of six, he hobbled into the Swan bar at Elmbury. Of his formidable appearance I have written elsewhere[1]: of his em-purpled cheeks, his nose like Bardolph's " an *ignis fatuus* or a ball of wildfire ", his deerstalker hat a pincushion for fishing-flies, his green Norfolk jacket and knee-breeches, his green stockings generally covered with burrs. Thus clad, he could stand still against a hedgerow and become part of the background, an Invisible Man: walking with him in rough country you got the impression that he appeared and disappeared at will, like some hobgoblin woodland spirit. But he was also the *genius loci* of the Swan; I doubt if he missed a morning or an evening session in a score of years. For the rest of the day he farmed in gentlemanly fashion, pottering round his fields with a gun under his arm, talking to labouring men about weathers and crops, leaning long upon gates, observing with a keen eye such hedgerow happenings as the pursuit of a rabbit by a stoat, the abundance or scarcity of berries, the hatching out of this butterfly or the blossoming of that familiar flower. His life passed so uneventfully, being like Gilbert White's ' untroubled by any vicissitudes other than those of the seasons ', that you might think it a wonder he had anything new to talk about when he came to the Swan for his midday beer or his six o'clock whisky. In fact there was never a morning when he didn't have some news for us; never an evening when he failed to bring us a lively tale of something surprising, curious, outlandish or puzzling that had beguiled his hours. He would tell us of a battle of wits between himself and the magpies, jays, carrion crows or rickyard rats against which he waged a desultory Thirty Years' War; or he would describe the ingenious architecture of a long-tailed tit's nest built in a blackthorn; or entertain us with a tale about how Sweep, his

[1] *Portrait of Elmbury* and *Brensham Village*.

Labrador, caught the moles which were making oontitoomps on his lawn. He would also turn out his pockets, or his haversack, upon the bar counter and exhibit to us his finds or his victims: an extra-long eel to affright the barmaid, or confined in a match-box a death's head hawk moth caterpillar he'd discovered on his potatoes ("Oh Colonel, there you go with your creepy-crawlies again!"). Or he'd show us a grass-snake's sloughed-off skin which he'd picked up on a hedge-bank, or one of those 'dollies' of twisted straw which his thatcher had fashioned in an idle moment when he had finished the rick, or an owl's pellet he'd found under the oak-tree on his lawn, or a stag-beetle with its remarkable horns, or a red underwing moth he'd spotted sitting on a telegraph-pole. His old eyes didn't miss much as he pottered about his farm; more than anybody I have ever met he was deserving of the epitaph which Thomas Hardy wrote for himself in a poem of his later days:

'*He was a man who used to notice such things*'.

So INTO the Swan at the stroke of six he hobbles in my memory still, upon a night in the backend season when dusk falls before opening-time and we are apt to remark how the evenings are drawing in. He carries an air of the autumn about him: mud on his boots, burrs on his stockings, wind-whipped berry-red face. He dumps in a corner his fishing-rod and landing-net and up to the counter he stumps for his usual large whisky, bearing upon a piece of string threaded through its gills a five-pound pike which ignoring the barmaid's protests he plops down upon the bar.

"There you are!" he says. "The first of the season; I tiddled him out with a minnie. Never in twenty years have I failed to catch my first pike on October Fair Day!"

Fair Day is the twelfth of October; and the Colonel, who was one of those men who make their own traditions, always insisted that this was the proper opening of the pike-fishing season. He'd have felt something had gone wrong with the world if he had failed to catch a pike on that day. Moreover, after the fish had been duly

13

admired in the Swan he always had it cooked by his long-suffering sisters according to the old recipe of Izaak Walton, which involves the use of thyme, marjoram, winter savory, claret, quantities of butter, oranges and garlic. The recipe pleasantly ends: "This dish of meat is too good for any but anglers, or very honest men; and I trust you will prove both, and therefore I have entrusted you with this secret."

For my part I am not very fond of any of our coarse-fish; but the Colonel was of an experimental turn of mind and on principle he ate everything he caught, pike, roach, dace, bream and chub, as well as eels, which he flavoured with nutmeg. Walton's *Compleat Angler*, and the Bible on Sundays, were the only two books he ever read, and so it had come about that the *Compleat Angler* shared a little of the Biblical authority in his mind; he insisted that his sisters should carry out its culinary instructions to the letter and he even went to the length of eating a dish called Minnow Tansy, which consists of minnows fried in the yolk of eggs with the flowers of cowslips and primroses and a little tansy. This prettily-named delicacy took him six months to prepare; for tansy is a herb of the late summer but primroses and cowslips, of course, can only be had in the spring. So in August he collected the flower heads of the tansy, dried them, and stored them away until April; then he gathered cowslips and primroses and set forth, with a disproportionate amount of tackle, to catch minnows in his brook. This was as if an eagle should descend to catching flies; for the Colonel had shot lions in Africa and elephants in India, he'd caught mahseer in the Tigris and salmon on Deeside and trout in the Test. However he set himself a target of a hundred minnows, which he attained after four hours' serious fishing, and since there was a good deal of the schoolboy in him still he enjoyed himself very much. He also enjoyed his supper, and agreed with Izaak Walton that it was 'a most dainty dish of meat'.

He would try anything. Somebody told him that if you ate a pigeon a day for a week the cumulative effect would kill you; so the Colonel shot, and ate, a pigeon a day for a week and on the seventh day walked triumphantly into the bar declaring "Well, I beyunt jud, be I?" He often lapsed into Gloucestershire, partly in fun, partly I think unconsciously. He had been born on the family farm to which he came back in his retirement; and he had learned the country speech from his father's carter and cowman, when he was a boy.

He was even more recklessly experimental with fungi than he was with pigeons. He had learned to recognise the Death Cap, which is called *phalloides* for an obvious reason, but he ate every other sort, "to see what they tasted like". He did this with confidence, holding that whisky was an antidote to all other poisons. Before eating a supper of toadstools, the bright orange sort, fried, he took the precaution of having an extra drink or two. "That'll quell 'em," he said, "that'll keep 'em quiet!" On the evening I am thinking of, when the pike lay on the counter regarding us with a toothy and avaricious expression reminiscent of certain horse-dealers', he showed us the puffballs with which he proposed to garnish it. He brought them out of his haversack, that cornucopia which poured forth so many strange things in the Swan bar, and the last of them was an enormous puffball, as big as a round Dutch cheese. "Bound to be tasty," he said, "a puffball as big as that un." And he ordered another whisky, just to be on the safe side.

From the bottom of the haversack, the last exhibit of the evening, he produced a curiosity and laid it on the bar beside the pike. It was a parti-coloured mole caught by his dog Sweep, whose method of catching moles was to stand upon the lawn, with his head cocked on one side, until he heard a mole working in its burrow, and then to stalk it, treading very softly, until he was near enough to pounce. His pounce always brought him to the exact spot where the mole was burrowing; his forefeet and his long sharp nose went through the crumbling soil together; a second later he was tossing the dead mole over his shoulder. He enjoyed this sport as much as a day's shooting; and since he had no further interest in the moles when he had killed them, and they were hardly marked by the snap of his jaws, the Colonel soon had enough to make a moleskin coat, which I think takes about 250. But the Colonel's moles were more various than most people's; and he was very proud of this eccentricity. Now and then, instead of the usual grey-black pelt with its pewtery sheen, the coat they wore was yellow or sandy, the colour of Tamworth pigs. He swore to us indeed that he had seen a pink one ("and that was before I took to drinking dam' near a bottle a day"). But this pied specimen, part sandy, part black, was something new even to the Colonel: and of course it made him more proud of his moles than ever.

"Pretty little beggar; I never saw the like of it in all my days. Well, *he'll* make no more oontitoomps on my lawn!"

I can almost hear him saying 'oontitoomps', dwelling with enjoyment upon the word; for he delighted in the speech of countrymen and in its unlettered poetry, and as I have said he always talked best when he let himself fall into it, using quite naturally his labourers' quirks of grammar and turns of phrase. Indeed the very last sentence he spoke to me was framed in such a fashion; when the angina was sharp in his chest, and the doctor had told him he'd never again be able to potter about his fields, he told me with a grin:

"John, I'd as lief be jud."

Lief: willingly. As Shakespeare used it, and as Englishmen have always used it when their speech has been uncorrupted by society fashions, University affectations, suburban 'refinement', and the B.B.C.; as Housman used it most beautifully, recollecting perhaps some Shropshire Lad's talk at Clungunford or Clun:

> *If man could live forever*
> *With liquor, love and fights,*
> *Lief would I rouse at mornings*
> *And lief lie down at nights.*

And lief would I be in the Swan again hearing the Colonel say 'oontitoomps', which of course were the molehills which disfigured his lawn. A learned judge, not long ago, heard the word spoken in his court during the trial of some agricultural case;

he was duly astonished, and wrote to *The Times* about it. But an oont is a mole all over England (except in a few places where they prefer to call it a mouldywarp), and its little hills of course are tumps. They are a nuisance when they come up in your garden, but I think I detect a sort of affectionate amusement in the word oontitoomps. One can often hear in a country word the echo of a laugh, or see in its appearance the shadow of a smile. ' Mum-ruffin' is a particularly endearing example of this; it is the nickname we give to the long-tailed tit, and the Colonel, of course, when he found those purse-shaped beautifully tailored nests in the sloe-bushes, always spoke of ' the clever little mumruffins' that made them. It sounds like a word invented by children. Actually a lot of country words probably owe their origin to the quick vision of a child, seeing something for the first time, seeing it *brand-new*. For instance, it was clearly a schoolboy who first called the Yellow-hammer the ' Scribbling Schoolmaster', because of the hieroglyphic markings upon its eggs. The Colonel, however, called it ' the Writing Lark'; and sometimes he would bring one of its eggs into the Swan to show us, saying " Look at the writing on it: just like the prescriptions that damned old sawbones writes out for me! " He never took the medicine of course; he ' poured it down the sink and had an extra whisky instead'. By these and other expedients he contrived to live to seventy and to die at that age without fuss or lingering, so saving himself from the years of crippledom that would have broken his heart.

HOWEVER, at the time I am writing about he was hale enough to spend a morning mole-catching, an afternoon pike-fishing, an evening whisky-drinking, and then to have a look round the October Fair on the way home. He picked up his mole and his puff-balls, and stowed them in the filthy old haversack which was coated inside with assorted feathers and fur, dried blood, and the crusted slime of eels; he collected his fishing-rod and net; and dangling his pike from its string he set off to see if the Mop, as we called it, was as merry an affair as it used to be in his boyhood. In his deerstalker hat, beneath which his hobgoblin face burned like a brazier, in his Norfolk breeches and his leaf-green stockings, with the wicked-looking pike swinging at his side, he must have looked more of a raree-show than most of the raree-shows which advertised themselves in the light of the naphtha-flares, along the High Street, down Church Street, and up the Barton Road. If he entered any of the booths I dare say their Hairy Women and Fat Boys gazed back at him with a greater wonder than he felt as he stared at them.

II

THE GATHERING DARKNESS of the backend season is stabbed and shot through with these bright lights: the whirling constellations of the merry-go-rounds at the Fair, the bonfires and Roman candles and rockets of Guy Fawkes' Day, and then at last the shine and the warm glow of Christmas. It's as if like ancient tribesmen we burn fires to keep winter and its wolves at bay; and indeed we are hardly ever aware of winter until Christmas has come and gone.

Elmbury's Mop Fair is a pool of light indeed. You can see the loom of it from six miles away, and you can imagine how it must have looked to ploughboys as they tramped in their best clothes towards it, fifty years ago when there were few street-lights, no car-lights, and winter nights were as black as those we knew only at the darkest hour of the last war.

The Fair survives against all probability, defying cut-throat competition from all the modern forms of fun. It draws its vigour, I think, from some old boisterousness which slumbers within us, a demon with whom we have made a private bargain, that it will lie easy on condition we let it loose upon this one night of the year. Occasional orgies are salutary, as priests and psychologists know. At the Fair men who would otherwise perhaps smash up the home can pay sixpence for the privilege of violently throwing balls at coconuts or old crockery or bottles. Frustrated motorists, bumping and boring in the dodgem cars, can get rid of the inhibitions which the Law and good manners have imposed upon them, and indulge in head-on collisions without hurt. Children whose parents are fussy about their digestions make themselves sick for once with a glorious mixture of hot-dogs and fairy-floss. J.P.'s and Councillors, even the Mayor himself, ride on the roundabouts and revolve giddily on the swings and slide down the chute to land in a heap with giggling wenches. As for the boys and girls who sit side by side in the little airborne carriages whizzing above our heads, nobody knows what mischief they get up to; and on Fair Day nobody cares.

But I do notice that all of us, as we grow older, are apt to pronounce on the day following the Fair that " of course it isn't what it was "; whereas of course it is we who are not what we were:

> *The pence are here, and here's the Fair,*
> *But where's the lost young man?*

As FOR Guy Fawkes' Day, perhaps its survival is even more remarkable than the persistence of our old-fashioned Fair; for this is surely a very strange and delightful quirk of the human character, that in a world of big bangs we are not yet bored with little ones. When you come to think of it, is it not surprising that we can tolerate bangs at all? Our generation has been plagued with bangs. We have been deafened from time to time by barrages, flying bombs, rockets, land and sea mines, supersonic thunderclaps; we have seen great cities laid waste by fire; we have read in the papers of atomic explosions comparable with volcanic eruptions; we await almost with resignation the Final Bang of all. Yet we still spend sixpence on a squib to celebrate Guy Fawkes' Day.

Now the old Colonel, whose daring empiricism I have told you of, used to celebrate it in a fashion which is properly discouraged by all prudent people. He would take several copies of *The Farmer and Stockbreeder*, roll them up to make a thick cylinder, wire them tightly, fill the space in the middle with gun-powder obtained by cutting the tops off old and unreliable sporting cartridges, fit a long fuse, plug the ends securely, and then achieve a bigger bang than anybody in those days could have bought for five shillings. The ostensible purpose was to entertain the children of his village; the real purpose I suppose was to entertain himself. The children at any rate were equally entertained whether the thing went off or whether it didn't. They would no doubt have enjoyed it still more if (to adapt Hilaire Belloc):

> *A Smell of Burning filled the Upper Air:*
> *The Firework-maker was no longer there!*

I used to assist the Colonel at some of these pyromaniac exhibitions. The preparations took all day. It was his custom to pile the prunings from his fruit trees around their trunks, where they provided harbour for rabbits; so in the morning of Guy Fawkes' Day his men were employed to remove these faggots and build a huge bonfire, while we stood by shooting the rabbits which bolted from the heaps. This operation went on until lunch-time, when we drank some very powerful cherry-brandy which the Colonel nevertheless held to be a teetotal drink, so he laced it with some more brandy. This put him in the mood to fill the paper cylinders with the maximum amount of gunpowder. He sawed his old cartridges in two with a hacksaw and poured out the powder into an old pestle and mortar. Then he mixed with it any explosive stuff which it had occurred to him to buy at the chemist's. Then he decanted the powder into the rolled-up newspapers with a hand at least as generous as that with which he poured out his whisky.

At last dusk fell, the bonfire was lit, we had a drink or two, extra large ones in case, as he put it grinning, they should be our last on earth; the children arrived anticipatory and spectatorial, and the fun began. The Colonel, who had faced Afghan bullets and Zulu assagais, nevertheless treated his own fireworks with respect. Having lit the fuse, he fairly sprinted across the orchard; and the faster he went on his poor arthritic legs the greater was the anti-climax if the firework failed to explode. There was then a small sizzle, a hiss, and a flurry of sparks; sometimes a very faint derisory pop. It occurred to me when this happened that at least poor Guy Fawkes was spared the indignity, which such a figure of fun was surely destined for, of his barrels of gunpowder failing to explode. The odds are that they would have failed. There would have been, I think, a sort of woof, the barrels would have split,—a flash, a choking smoke, and out staggers Guy with his whiskers singed! Yet I have not read any history-book that has pointed out the child-like optimism of Messrs. Thomas Catesby, John Wright, Thomas Winter and Guy Fawkes, the cheerful assumption that with a contrivance of this sort they could blow up the whole of the Lords and Commons to say nothing of King James in his padded and dagger-proof doublet. No: Guy Fawkes was much more of a fool than he was a knave, and we with our instinctive sense of history are quite right to represent him as a figure of fun. Some learned historians have tried in vain to turn him into a tragic character; but the children with their soot-blackened faces and their " Penny for the Guy, Mister! " are better interpreters of history than the scholars. They commemorate him not as a tragic victim of circumstance, not as a black villain, but simply as a comic fool.

It was always last year's scarecrow that represented him on top of the Colonel's great bonfire. The Colonel made very good scarecrows; he exercised imagination upon them, he gave them mangel-wurzel heads and dressed them in the remnants of his military wardrobe. The last one I remember went to the stake wearing a sola topee. That was in 1938, the year before the Colonel died. There were no more bonfires in England after that, except the great ones made by the German airmen, until we lit the beacons on VE-day; but even they do not burn so bright in my memory as the crackling apple-boughs burned in the Colonel's orchard, with the Guy in the sola topee perched atop.

IN BETWEEN Bonfire Night and Christmas comes another festival, a local one, the Christmas Fat Stock Show and Sale. It is not quite so portentous an affair as it used to be, when as a child I watched Old Cookie and her minions cutting the mountains of sandwiches which would be provided free for the market-porters, drovers and hangers-on; for my father was an auctioneer. I shall never forget that sandwich-making, which went on for a whole day. Could there have been a thousand sandwiches? In retrospect it seems so. Mutton, ham, pork, cheese, roast beef—but the ones which stick in my memory were made of very thin slices of raw beef, peppered and mustarded, a carnivore's delight and a vegetarian's nightmare. I, at ten, was eagerly a carnivore; and it was a special treat to nibble one of these sandwiches which looked as if they contained tomato but were so much more exciting than that.

Our house looked out on to the main street down which all the traffic flowed on its way to the market. Even when I was very small I would sit at a front window all the morning watching the great Hereford steers waddling by, the pigs, the fat sheep under the netting in the drays, the farmers' wives driving in with their turkeys and geese. Later I would be allowed to walk up the side-road to the market itself to watch my father or my uncle selling the champion beast. How hugely that rosetted monster looms in my memory! The butcher who bought it would always lead it slowly round the town on the way to his slaughter-house; it was a good advertisement for him. I retain an impression of a butcher who was fat too, and a little short of wind so that in the chill air his breath, like the beast's, made a tiny cloud of steam that went before them both as they processed in triumph together down High Street, Church Street and Barton Road.

Indeed there was something Gargantuan about the whole Christmas Market scene. In my memory I see a plenitude of fat beasts and fat people. It was before the days of Dexadrine and dietary and doctors unlike Cæsar who would have everybody thin. The statisticians had not yet discovered that mere bags of bones have a better expectation of life than fat people; and fatness was regarded as an honourable rather than a dishonourable state. I remember the farmers' wives with loaded baskets, who swayed as they walked, themselves plump as dumplings; drovers who carried their sixteen stone a dozen miles before noon, a dozen miles home at night when the last pub had shut its doors; tubby ponies between the shafts of tubby floats; fat turkeys, geese and cockerels that the auctioneer's man would hold up clacking and squawking, " Feel its breast, Missus, feel its breast and see if you can touch the breast bone!" (How different from some of the Christmas geese which spivs sold us for fifty shillings just after the last war; of which the landlord of our local said " You could chuck 'em up in the air and they'd never come down again! ") Were pigs ever so fat as those Large Blacks, those Large Whites, those Saddlebacks of my childhood, when I would lean upon the iron pens and stare at them in wonder as if they were hippos? Even our native Gloster Spots, which when they run loose and get a thin living often achieve a resemblance to camels,—even they, properly fatted, were as fabulous beasts in a child's picture-book—they belonged to inn-signs rather than to real life.

And looming over all the fat Herefords: steaming, darkened with sweat till they were the colour of Herefordshire soil darkened by rain, moving in a mist of exhaled breath—and those butchers (surely all butchers then were fat and well-liking?) waddling among them, slapping huge haunches, running knowledgeable hands down wet flanks and over curly-haired withers!

When the legs and quarters and sirloins and undercuts appeared in the shops next week (shops lit more brightly, I fancy, at winter dusks than any shops are lit to-day) the First Prize rosette would be among them, and the name of the farmer who had fed the beast would be displayed: You bought not simply a sirloin but the sirloin from Mr. Pike's or Mr. Lane's champion. Maybe the farmer bought it himself; I like to think of his wife proudly cooking it, he proudly carving it, the whole large family proudly eating it, at the Christmas table.

Nowadays of course Gargantua is out of fashion. We grow smaller cattle, smaller sheep, and much smaller pigs. Our grandfathers, I suspect, would have been shocked at us for killing our pigs at nine score; they preferred something like the house-pig for which, a few years ago, I forgot to fill in the necessary form. An inflexible Ministry made me keep it for another four months by which time it weighed eighteen score.

My wife, rendering down the lard, gave herself a bilious attack;

24

and I ultimately cut out of the cured sides cubes of solid bacon fat six by six by twelve and gave them away to better men than I, who made their midday meal of doorsteps of bread, lumps of bacon fat, plenty of mustard, and a raw onion balanced on top of the edifice.

So as far as pigs go I think we are wiser than our forebears; but I doubt if our little pernickety pieces of roast beef and mutton can really match for flavour the great joints which were borne in, not by one pair of hands but by two, to the tables of our grandfathers. Small families, in the age of the Common Man, could not cope with them at all; we can only enjoy them if we are enormously philoprogenitive, or if we get ourselves sent to reformative institutions, or on special occasions of rejoicing or celebration, such as the Cricket Club dinner or the Coronation Feast.

LEST YOU should imagine that all good eating is a thing of the past in our part of the country, I must digress to tell you about the Coronation Feast which was held at Brensham's Norton in 1953. Brensham lies about four miles north of Elmbury, and Brensham's Norton is a kind of offshoot from it, a hamlet merely, consisting of a few farms, a church, a sizeable house or two, a cluster of cottages, and a fine old Tithe Barn, which is just the place for dances, whist drives, dinners and events of that kind.

Now Brensham's Norton, in celebrating the Coronation, did all that was needful and proper. It decorated itself; it gave mugs to all the children under the age of twelve; it organised a tug of war across the Avon in the course of which the losing team was pulled in; its inhabitants dutifully went to church on Sunday and doubtless listened to the Queen's speech on the wireless. But the main item in the celebrations, it must be admitted, was a supper, attended by the 151 members of the adult population, for which the most careful and loving preparations were made. Beer was brought to the Village Hall and racked several days beforehand: two casks of 36 gallons each were deemed, after exact calculations, to be barely sufficient; so a reserve supply of bottled beer was provided as well.

ι twelve-score pig, a fat lamb, and a fat calf were killed and duly ooked; and of course there was a sufficiency of vegetables to go vith the meat, as well as plenty of roly-poly puddings, bread and heese and so on, to fill any empty corners. On Coronation Night he 151 villagers met together and sat down to this repast. It did ιot occur to them until about half-way through the meal that hey were making only the slightest impression upon it; but then hey became very concerned indeed and said to each other: " Us'll ιever finish it all! What shall us do?" At last a sensible fellow ιuggested " Let us sit down here again to-morrow evening at the ιame time." This brilliant idea was much applauded; and the ;ollowing day, at 8 p.m., the gallant 151 gathered together to deal with the remains of a twelve-score pig, a fat lamb, a fat calf and what they airily called " the oddments." But by nine-thirty they were again asking each other " What shall us do?" for they were full to bursting and the trestles still sagged under their load of viands. " We carsn't meet again *to-morrow*," they said, " 'Twouldnt' look nice."

" 'Twould be held against us," they agreed.

So in the end it was decided to meet again on the Saturday; when I am assured that after an interval of fasting they polished off every scrap that was left, leaving no more than a few bones for the hens to pick and a morsel or two for the Tithe Barn cat.

I, WHO have never been addicted to great feastings, am nevertheless fascinated by gluttony; I have a sneaking admiration for those mighty trenchermen who like Nicholas Wood, a yeoman of Kent in the 17th century, " did eat with ease a whole sheep of 16 shillings price, at a meal." My admiration for him is somewhat lessened when I read that he ate it raw. " Another time," declares his chronicler, " he did eat 13 dozen of pigeons." (13 x 12—and by Gargantua! that's 156!) " At Sir William Sedley's he did eat as much as would have sufficed 30 men; at my Lord Wotton's in Kent, he did eat at one meal 84 rabbits, which number would have sufficed 168 men. He suddenly devoured 18 yards of black pudding,

London measure——" I like that "suddenly"; clearly he was an impulsive fellow; he put away 18 yards of black pudding as absentmindedly as we might gobble a cocktail-biscuit. "Having once eaten 60 lbs weight of cherries, he said they were but waste-meat. He made an end of a whole hog at once, and after it swallowed three pecks of damsons; this was after breakfast, for he said he had ate one bottle of milk, one of pottage, with bread, butter and cheese before. 'He did eat in my presence,' saith Taylor the water-poet, '6 penny wheaten loaves, 3 sixpenny veal pies, 1 pound of sweet butter, one good dish of thornback,'". —this was skate or ray, I think— "' and a sliver of a fresh household loaf, an inch thick, and all this within the space of an hour; the house yielded no more, so he went away unsatisfied. . . .' "

The story ends sombrely. "He spent all his estate to provide for his belly; and though a landed man, and a true labourer, he died very poor in 1630."

You will observe that he died not of overeating but presumably of starvation; and it is very sad indeed to think of this poor fellow being so hard put to it to find the wherewithal to buy a mere 18 yards or so of black pudding for his snack between meals. He should have taken a tip from Apicius, the Roman gourmand, whose income being reduced to £80,000 by reason of his luxurious living, committed suicide rather than face the necessity to subsist on a plain and frugal diet.

NORTON's Coronation Feast went unrecorded in the columns of our local weekly; the participants were, to tell the truth, a little embarrassed about it. "'Twill be held against us," they said. But in the past people had no such inhibitions and were proud, even boastful, of their vast eating and drinking. Turning over the files of our weekly paper, I came across elaborate accounts of great Christmas banquets held in aid of this and that, with the twelve-course menus printed in full. Sometimes we are even told how much beer, port or wine was consumed, for this seems to have been a matter of general interest in the middle of the 19th century, as we readily learn from the novels of Dickens. In an issue of 1840 there is an item which fascinates me. A regiment of soldiers marched through the town; and in no time £46 had been collected for " their entertainment with bread and cheese and beer." Now I believe that beer in those days cost about twopence a pint; and a regiment did not consist of more than 500 men. Bread and cheese cannot have been very expensive; so a rough calculation suggests that the redcoats must have drunk about 50 pints apiece in the course of their two-days' stay! Possibly, however, some of the locals shared the beer; for in an adjoining column to the story of the soldiers' visit is an account of how an engine-driver " being in a considerable state of intoxication " ran down and killed two gangers on the newly-opened branch line at Elmbury. He was later charged with manslaughter and was acquitted, " the Grand Jury having ignored the bill preferred against him." There are some curious aspects of this story. For instance the inhabitants of Elmbury, who seem to have had a passion for public subscriptions, not only raised a fund for the benefit of the gangers' widows and children but also contributed handsomely " to defray the cost of the engine-driver's defence." Why they did so, and why the Grand Jury threw out the bill, remains a mystery. Possibly to be drunk in charge of a Puffing-Billy seemed almost romantic in 1840. Indeed I can feel a little sympathy for the engine-driver myself. Thirty miles an hour, and sparks flying out of the tall smokestack! Horses and cows galloping away madly at the sight of the snorting monster! The furnace glowing red, and the drink afire in the engine-driver's belly! I doubt if any of the jet-pilots whose machines scream over our heads get as much of a thrill out of their 500 m.p.h. as that engineman did out of his last, drunken drive.

THE BEER, of course, was stronger in those days; or so we are always being told. But turning over the pages of John Nyren's *Cricketers of My Time* which was written about 1840 I find him complaining bitterly about the swipes which was then sold under the name of ale. He is describing a match he played as a youth, between the

Men of Hambledon and All England. "How these fine, brawn-faced fellows of farmers would drink to our success!" he exclaims, and goes on to tell us what they used to drink. "Punch! Not your modern cat-lap milk punch—punch bedevilled—but good, unsophisticated John Bull stuff—stark!—that would stand on end—punch that would make a cat speak! Sixpence a bottle! The ale too!—not the modern horror under the same name, that drives as many men melancholy-mad as the hypocrites do—not the beast-liness of these days, that will make a fellow's inside like a shaking bog—and as rotten; but barley-corn, such as would put the souls of three butchers into one weaver. Ale that would flare like turpentine—genuine Boniface!"

We'll forgive him the superfluity of exclamation marks if the beer was as good as all that. But let us turn now to the Welsh bard Sion Tudor, who was also extremely fond of beer and who wrote his poems about three hundred years before Nyren was born. He held that the only beer which was worth drinking was the beer he had drunk in *his* own youth; but as for the stuff they give you nowadays, he said, (nowadays being about 1560) why it's enough to make a poet sick. Almost every time he called at an inn he was inspired by nausea to make up a poem about the bad beer, which he scrawled with a quartz upon the window-pane as a warning to wayfarers who might follow him, thus:

> *Chester ale! Chester ale! I could ne'er get it down.*
> *'Tis made of ground ivy, of dirt, and of bran.*
> *'Tis as thick as a river below a huge town!*
> *'Tis not lap for a dog, far less drink for a man!*

Ground ivy, that little creeping herb with purplish-blue flowers, was used for flavouring ale—for making it 'bitter'—before the use of hops became common; and even after that by brewers who thought the purchase of hops was an unnecessary extravagance. George Borrow, walking through Wales in the footsteps of Sion Tudor, had the misfortune to call at an inn where the landlady was of such a cheese-paring nature, and where the beer brewed with ground ivy was almost as sharp as wormwood.

" ' This is very bad ale,' I said.

" ' It ought to be very good,' said she, ' for I brewed it myself.'

" So I told her: ' The goodness of ale does not so much depend upon who brews it as on what it is brewed of.' "

One up to George Borrow. But isn't it strange that these three hearty beer-drinkers who flourished at different times, the great cricketer, the peripatetic bard, and the author of *Lavengro*, should *each* have held the view that the beer of their youth was as nectar compared with the cat-lap of their later years? " A modern horror," said John Nyren in the 1840's; " Thick as a river," said Sion Tudor some fifty years before Shakespeare created Falstaff; " Wormwood," snapped George Borrow, in 1860; and so on. And I'm prepared to bet that if I go down to the pub to-night and get into conversation with the old men, it will not be very long before I hear three or four familiar phrases which fall from their lips as inevitably as the leaves fall from the trees every autumn.

" Evenin's be drawing in," they'll say.

" Ah."

" Christmas seems to come round quicker every year," they'll say.

" 'Tis so as we git older."

" Christmas ain't what it was."

" Nor's the beer neither. Swipes! Cat-lap! Ditch-water and chemicals! Why, when I was a lad . . ."

Now as a postscript to all those seasonable tales of eating and drinking, here is the story of the most expensive meal ever paid for by four jolly farmers who live near Elmbury, Dave, Jack, William and Thomas. They are all fatstock men, breeders of Herefords, and last December they went up, for the first time, to the Smithfield Show. When the show was over they got into mischief and after various wanderings round the West End of London found themselves in a Night Club. The management of the Club apparently recognised them for what they were—and no wonder, for they are all huge red-faced fellows who walk (and no doubt dance) with the air of men who have several pounds of West Midland mud on their boots. At any rate the band was instructed to play " For to be a Farmer's Boy " at which my friends, touched by the tribute, bought champagne all round. Shortly four pretty dance-hostesses joined them at their table. These dutiful girls submitted to having their feet trodden on by the dancing farmers, whose own feet are like the plodding hoofs of Shire horses; and between dances they refreshed themselves with Pineapple Specials, blameless and teetotal concoctions; for dance-hostesses have to be abstemious since they are on duty every night until 4 a.m. The farmers, of course, continued to drink champagne. Towards 2 o'clock, growing hungry, they ordered eggs and bacon. The portions seemed insufficient, so they demanded a second helping. At 3 a.m., feeling sleepy, they asked for their bill.

The bill, carried by an obsequious waiter upon a silver tray, had the corner turned up, so that they had to unfold it to read the figures at the bottom. Having done so, they blinked. They were indeed, so staggered by the amount of the bill that they subsequently had only the faintest recollection of its details. Pineapple Specials, however, cost 15s. each; and the girls had lapped up Pineapple Specials with the determination of camels about to cross the thirsty Sahara. The eggs and bacon cost 17/6 a portion. There was a horrifying item: *Champagne for the Band.* . . . They clubbed together and paid the bill, and in their innocence offered to take the young women home by taxi; one lived in St. John's Wood, one in Kensington, one in Holland Park, and one in Camden Town. So the round journey was immensely long, expensive and by no means enlivened by the farmers' belated discovery that dance-hostesses were, contrary to their hopes and expectations, at least as prim and proper as the average clergyman's daughter.

Next day the farmers returned home. I met them that evening in the Swan, chastened and repentant, and drinking good honest beer at one and threepence a pint. When they had told me the

31

story I couldn't refrain from asking them exactly how much the whole trip had cost them. They pondered. They looked from one to the other, shy and somewhat embarrassed. At last Dave said:

" We reckoned it up. 'Twere an awful lot of money."

" But how much *did* it cost? " I persisted.

He hesitated. At last he told me:

" A bloody good bullock," he said.

I loved that. I thought how right it was, and how natural, to relate the cost of a silly spree to the real fundamental thing, the primary product. For money, after all, is only a symbol. The farmer got down to earth: literally. He matched the cost of the trip to London, railway fares, hotel bills, taxis, Pineapple Specials, Veuve Cliquot, dance-hostesses and all, with a deep-sided, red-coated, white-faced beast that had taken 30 months a-growing from calf to fat bullock: that had eaten so-much cattle cake and so-much silage, that had also cost so-much in men's wages to feed and care for it, so-much in straw, so-much in grazing. Its value would be about £75.

The four jolly farmers weren't grumbling. They'd had their fun and paid for it; they'd learned their lesson and remembered it; once bitten, twice shy. But unlike you and me, when we indulge in our comparable follies (though perhaps on a smaller scale), they thought of the money they'd spent in terms of what it really represented: what they'd had to produce to indulge in their spree; and, so they were brought face to face with a fact which most of us forget, that money doesn't descend upon Britain like manna from heaven, it is merely a means of exchange and a convenient equivalent for the things we manufacture and the things we grow.

III

THE HEDGES round about my home are shaggy now with old man's beard—a perfect country name incidentally for the wild clematis; its seed-heads in winter go grey and remind you, not indeed of the splendid snowy beards of Father Christmas and the late Mr. Bernard Shaw, but of some ancient tramp's unkempt whiskers hoar with frost upon a chilly morning. Of course the plant has another name, a sweet one, Traveller's Joy; and indeed it is a joy for all wayfarers who travel between the hedges,—all over England so long as there is lime in the soil.

But where the limestone or the chalk ceases, so abruptly does the old man's beard. You can draw for yourself a rough geological map by it; wherever it flourishes there is assuredly lime, just as wherever the foxglove grows there is assuredly little or none. These two plants are as opposite in their tastes as Jack Spratt and his missus. The foxglove is what the botanists call a calcifuge; it abhors lime. Wherever you find it growing happily you will be safe in planting rhododendrons and azaleas in your garden; for they too abominate an alkaline soil.

With or without the old man's beard, the hedges are lovely at this backend of the year. Berries of all kinds and every shade of colour make up for the absent flowers: claret-coloured haws and rose-hips orange-tawny, pink spindle and coral briony, with cuckoo-pint's red spikes—the reddest of all—flaunting themselves among the roots of the thorn. These are said to be poisonous—and so are the berries of the briony, but in my empirical youth I think I ate both and came to no harm. I have a fancy that we protected ourselves, when we were children, by the natural reaction of spitting out anything that tasted nasty. Few poisons, I think, are pleasant to the taste: Nature does not often practise that deceit upon us—it is only man, when he turns to poisoning, who smothers the dollop of weed-killer with the strawberry jam.

QUICK is the country name for the thorn which composes most of our hedgerows; we speak of a quickset hedge; and I dare say we use the word in both its senses, the thorn grows swiftly and the thorn is powerfully alive, almost indestructible, the Quick (in the Biblical sense) as opposed to the Dead. It is surely the native daemon of the English soil. It springs up everywhere, even through the tarmac runways of old abandoned aerodromes. The Life-force, whatever that may be, manifests itself in the hawthorn. If you say to yourself, I will have no hedge here, but seek nevertheless to part your field into two plots by means of a few strands of wire, you will shortly find a hedge flourishing against your will in the little space under the wire where your beasts cannot graze. Haw-thorn, indeed, helped to make the ancient forest floor of England; and a hedge is simply a fragment of the forest which is permitted to exist because it serves the ends of Man. Suppose you fall ill, or neglectful, or old, and you let your Naboth's Vineyard go out of cultivation for a twelve-months or more; sure enough the hedges will creep out again, out and out until all four hedges meet in the middle; the old indestructible Forest will come back. Truly we hold the countryside on sufferance from nature. If some fearful pandemic, some myxomatosis of mankind, were to decimate us, within two seasons the Forest would possess the land again, as it did before we learned to use our spades, our forks, our ploughs and above all our grazing beasts, to subjugate and hold it at bay.

HUNTING MEN say at this season that the country is ' blind ', a good phrase meaning that the hedges are still opaque with the dead or dying leaves; as you gallop up to them you cannot see what lies at the other side. Leaf-fall in the country is a very gradual process because there are so many different sorts of trees and shrubs dropping their leaves at different times between October and Christmas; but in a town where there are perhaps only plane trees, limes or chestnuts it is much more noticeable, sudden and somehow vaguely sinister. It was Shelley standing in the streets of Naples who

> *heard the autumnal leaves like light footfalls*
> *Of spirits passing through the streets.*

We can still hear it even in a modern city, when the traffic quietens at late evening and the lamps are lit and the big leaves of the plane trees float down soft as snow and are stirred on the pavements by some brief premonitory breath of winter. That small faint scuffling! It makes me imagine some scene from a Victorian novel, a pool of yellow gas-light, the faint clop-clop of a horse's hoofs, the distant rumble of a cab's wheels; shabby figures with coat-collars turned up passing to and fro, the huge silence of a city at night which vanished for ever when the internal combustion engine was invented. I see one of the muffled passers-by stop suddenly, and pause discomfortably, and listen. Shuffle-shuffle-shuffle go the leaves; and he quickens his pace and buries his ashen face deeper into his muffler, hearing at his heels some Victorian Nemesis. The girl he has betrayed, the partner he has cheated, the dying consumptive sister whom he has abandoned to let her starve? No, it is only the leaves. . . .

Alas for the vanished gas-light! Alas for the silence that is no more! When electricity and the petrol engine came in together, surely Melodrama made her last bow and withdrew for ever from the stage. The modern arc-lamps (which cause all of us to look a bit queer) show up her false make-up too clearly; and the roar and rattle of the buses drowns the terrible tiny patter of the footpad leaves.

THE LEAVES fall, each sort in a different fashion, according to their kind. Birch throws them down in golden handfuls like the sovereigns of Victorian days prodigally cast by some reformed Scrooge.

The elm, being so tall and giving its topsails to the strongest winds, streams out on gusty days a comet's tail of little leaves blown far and wide. The beech-leaves are brown already when they fall, and crisp, so that they drop upon the woodland floor with a faint harsh sound; they are reluctant to settle into earth's bosom and stay wakeful, stirring at the least breeze, agitated into dervish-dances like those dust-devils of the African sand.

The oak-leaves cling late, and are ripped off by the north-wester which brings the first snow. The ash-leaves spin down like minia-ture propellers whirling. The poplars spin too, but with a quicker rotation. The chestnut leaves float. On a still day, in a still church-yard, you can count the seconds as they fall; they are surely the 'falling leaves' which the early fliers imitated when they tried their first daring aerobatics, for they rock with a hammock's motion during their journey to the earth, a quick plunge, a slower ascent, a stall, a spin, a plunge, an ascent, until at last with quite an audible plop they fall on to the wet pavement where they lie so deep that they are over the tops of your shoes as you scuffle through them. So the man who looks after the churchyard must sweep them away, or the rain will turn them to mush, and the old folk next Sunday will grumble and wish for the goloshes which were fashion-able in their youth, and the young ones will find a peculiar delight in sliding among them, so that they pile up in wet heaps over the tops of their shoes,—" Come *along*, Tommy, whatever are you doing, you'll catch your death, with your stockings all soaked, sitting through the sermon . . ."

OLD people hate dead leaves, and forget, most strangely, the pleasure which in youth they had with them; just as they forget the joy of snow, and think only of the slush. When we played Babes in the Wood games long ago, upon the beechwood carpet that was loud with the brown leaves stirring and rough with the mast, we never thought " There's another year gone by." But the old think so; and with a little shiver they look up, and see the brown flecks and the yellow falling, falling out of the grey sky, at this sad sweet season which always brings to my mind those sad sweet lines by John Webster:

> *Call for the robin redbreast and the wren*
> *Since o'er the shady groves they hover,*
> *And with leaves and flowers do cover*
> *The friendless bodies of unburied men.* . . .

Now the evergreens come into their own; and we are glad even of the ivy which creeps everywhere over my walls and climbs up the house among the wistaria and the honeysuckle. The bees are glad of it too. Whenever we have a mild spell there is a buzzing about it as loud as summer's, and I see scores of honeybees, with some late wasps and a multitude of flies, feeding on the nectar which lies in the little green flowers. At night, if I take a look at the ivy by torchlight, I find a swarm of moths feeding there, mostly drab or sable or chestnut ones, but among them a few that have their upperwings beautifully patterned with orange-pink. This quite common moth is called The Herald; it looks exotic in the torchlight, out of place in England in November. Being a hibernator, it must feed on what it can get before the frosts come, to store up some sustenance against the long months of sleep. The ivy ramping over old tree-trunks in the rough patch at the bottom of the garden, provides it with the last sweets of the year.

I am told I should at least make an effort to tame and discipline my ivy. It will damage the walls, it will make the house damp, it "harbours" slugs, it "harbours" snails. And so it may; but the truth is that I love ivy, I love the shield-shape of its dark leaves and the grace of its long tendrils, it is associated in my mind with Greece and Rome and the poetry men made when the world was young. I think of Swinburne's

> *The ivy falls from the Bacchanal's hair*
> *Over her eyebrows hiding her eyes.*

I think of Pan and the wanton nymphs and the swiftfoot Satyrs chasing them through woodland glades; and the altars of old gods, and the grave bearded priests, and the wild splendid pæan lifted from a thousand throats upon some day of triumph or festival.

I think of Lycidas, too:

> *Yet once more, O ye laurels, and once more*
> *Ye myrtles brown, with ivy never sere. . . .*

No: I shall keep my ivy, until it digs its cunning little claws deep into the mortar of my walls and begins to pull brick from brick, which assuredly it will do, being the servant of the woodland gods and having no love for the habitations of man.

But all good gardeners hate it; they hate anything which may possibly ' harbour ' anything, snails, moths, mice, caterpillars, woodlice, 'Arry-long-legs and what they call Erri-wigs. So apprehensive are gardeners of their multitudinous foes that I honestly believe they are only truly happy when they have dug up every vegetable thing and achieved a large empty space consisting entirely of bare brown earth, most excellently tilled. This is the time of year when they can, for a brief space, indulge in this pleasure. No weeds grow. They dig the ground, they fork it over; and then they lean upon their fork-handles and they are happy for a space, contemplating the bare patch, slugless, snailless, erri-wigless, though incidentally plantless too. They do not mind that; for they love green things less than they hate the ' pestses ' which devour them.

Women, even the best of wives, agree with gardeners in loathing ivy. They too hate slugs, snails, 'Arry-long-legs, erri-wigs, woodlice, though for different reasons: they hate them because they give them the creeps. Also they have provident minds and hate to think of walls crumbling in the grip of the lovely clinging wanton plant. Moreover, they are possessed by the notion of tidiness, they delight in snipping and pruning and clipping and trimming, as did Her late Majesty Queen Mary, whose memory we revere. But she too hated ivy. It is said she would assail it personally, with shears in her gloved hands; she would sever its stems, and rip it from the walls; and even if she were staying in some subject's house she would seek permission to attack the ivy, her ladies-in-waiting standing dutifully by, she formidably armed with the clippers and the well-oiled shears. It would have been a bold and impudent ivy that would dare to put forth the tiniest tendril after receiving so stern a reproof from so magnificent a lady as she was.

IV

SOME WINTRY PICTURES hung appropriately upon the walls of the Swan bar in the days when the Colonel used to come in hoar and half-frozen after standing knee-deep in flood-water waiting for duck. They represented the exploits of John Mytton, and the Colonel never tired of them, for he had a fellow-feeling for one who would stalk wild duck across a frozen lake by moonlight, clad only in his night-shirt; it was the kind of thing he might have done himself in his young days. He particularly liked the picture of Mytton setting fire to his night-shirt ' to frighten his damned hiccups away'; and of course he loved the very lively Alken drawing of Mytton riding into his dining-room upon the back of a bear, a feat which he undertook in order to frighten the tame clergyman who was a supernumerary of his large household, holding a position in the establishment somewhat similar to that of the tame bear. The Colonel, who disliked parsons on principle, much as Cobbett did, used to chuckle over this picture, rejoicing in the cleric's discomfiture. " Look at the dam' feller, climbing up on the table! "

Then there was the print which showed the famous gig episode. Mytton was tearing along a country lane with a timid passenger who protested at the pace.

" Was you ever much hurt, then, by being upset in a gig? " asked Squire Mytton.

" No, thank God," answered the passenger, " for I never was upset in one."

" What? " cried Mytton. " Never upset in a gig? What a damned slow fellow you must have been all your life! "—and with that he ran the near wheel up the bank and over they went, horse, gig and all. The damned slow fellow was not seriously hurt, and subsequently with astonishing fortitude he married Mytton's daughter. If he hoped for an inheritance, he was unlucky; for Mytton succeeded in getting rid of half a million pounds in fifteen years, which took a bit of doing in those days if one's extravagances were of the more or less normal kind, e.g. drink, horses, gambling and girls. Unfortunately Mytton added some extraordinary prodigalities of his own. He had a curious objection to paper money, and to demonstrate his contempt for it he would sometimes *eat* a five pound note laid upon a piece of bread and butter. Or he would throw away wads of £100 or so as he walked round his estate; or he would let a thousand or two blow out of his coach on a windy night as he came spanking home from the races.

He decided to stand for Parliament, and rode through Shrewsbury, his chosen constituency, handing out £10 notes to anybody who held forth a hand. The election cost him £10,000 and he duly went to Westminster. He spent exactly half an hour in the House of Commons, which he decided was stuffy and dull. So he came home, and resumed his fox-hunting. He never went to the House again.

Instead he took to drinking six bottles of port a day, for which in his later years he substituted six bottles of brandy. His end was sad and no doubt satisfactory to the moralists; for he whose days had been spent in the pursuit of almost every conceivably huntable creature was now himself hunted by his creditors up and down the length and breadth of England. He escaped for a time to Calais (" with a couple of bum-baillies hard on his brush "); and it was while he was there, being troubled one night by the hiccups, that he set his night-shirt on fire. He was severely burned, but he bore the pain with stoical courage, writing from what he truly believed to be his death-bed self-mocking notes to his friends,—in which, incidentally, he correctly quoted Horace, Sophocles and the Bible in Greek! He must have had a remarkable memory, for I doubt if he had ever read a book since his schooldays.

'When at last urgent business, or nostalgia, or merely whim brought him back to England his creditors gathered about him once more. He was arrested and imprisoned at the King's Bench in London; and there he died, in *delirium tremens*, at the age of 38.

He was crazy, useless, profligate—I give you all that; yet his galloping career surely has its moments of wild splendour. "Light come, light go" is the title of Alken's picture of the bank notes blowing out of the coach. It is a moonlight night, and windy, with ragged clouds chasing each other across the moon. The four horses, as usual, are at full gallop. The money streams out behind the coach like the paper tail of a boy's kite; and within sits Mytton uncaring. There are people who believe money to be something sacred; and the print must shock those people profoundly. Bank Managers, I am sure, would like to put it upon an *Index Expurgatorius*. But for my part I like a man who throws money away better than one who counts it three times before he goes to bed; and so I have a soft spot in my heart for the memory of poor Jack Mytton.

I'VE A SOFT SPOT too—who hasn't?—for Alken's delightful prints. Most of all I like his aquatints of gentlemen out shooting in top-hats, cutaway coats and (one would think) unsuitable trousers, pursuing ducks, pheasants and hares in bright and snowy weather. The artist always makes his one concession to the dramatic moment and to his subject's self-esteem; for each muzzle-loader that has been fired there is at least one mallard or cock-pheasant in a flurry of feathers tumbling out of the sky. Likewise in the fishing-prints the angler is always attended by a dutiful keeper carrying the net, the creel and the inevitable brace of trout or pike; for there were no blank days in that beautiful aquatinted world of Alken.

You will notice too that in the hunting-pictures of the period the running hounds are always so tightly packed that, as foxhunters say in their pleasant hyperbole, "You could cover them with a handkerchief." And this, I suppose, was the artist's necessary compliment to the M.F.H. who had commissioned the painting and whose hounds in real life perhaps straggled over half his hunting-country and ran riot chasing rabbits, hares and old maids' tabbies. Perhaps the plenitude of falls which are shown in these pictures was a kind of compliment too, suggesting what devil-may-care fellows the riders were. At any rate the artist was always at pains to show some examples of what was called " Grief." Somebody had to fall, and generally to smash the top of a five-barred gate in the course of doing so.

The red fox streaking across the field, the eager hounds at his brush, and of course the horses, are always shown with their forelegs stretched out forward, their hindlegs stretched out behind, and the belly close to the ground. No living creature gallops like this; and it has been ingenuously suggested that until the invention of railway-trains, from which fast-moving passengers could observe the movements of fast-moving creatures running parallel with themselves, people really believed that horses galloped in such a fashion. This of course is sheer nonsense; so is the idea that photography suddenly demonstrated to man something which his own eye had always been too slow to perceive. In fact, the human eye acts more quickly than did the best Victorian cameras; and many painters drew horses correctly—that is to say, as *we* see them—hundreds of years ago. It was, I think, simply a convention in the 18th and early 19th century to paint horses *ventre à terre*: it seemed to make them move faster. And so we see a coach with every one of its team stretched out in this unnatural way going like billy-o from London to Birmingham. And we see the Midnight Steeplechasers in that ubiquitous set of prints, streaking through the night on steeds that would surely have split themselves if they had really galloped so.

The first midnight steeplechase took place near Ipswich. The riders were some of the officers of a cavalry regiment quartered there; the prints show them with blue trousers bearing a yellow stripe. They wore, by agreement, night-shirts and night-caps; and the prints capture most perfectly the ghostly moonlight pallor shining on the night-caps as the horsemen tore across country in that crazy race, slap across country from the barracks to some church that had a visible spire. Six finished; and in the last print we see them galloping down the village street, singing " The Lads of the Village ", hollering and whooping, with all the inhabitants, night-shirted and holding candles, leaning out of their windows and cheering the winner. Would they cheer nowadays? They would probably complain to the police, or write to the papers about the ill-behaviour of the Idle Rich disturbing the well-deserved slumbers of the Workers.

THE SWAN was an old coaching house; and pride of place among the pictures in the bar was given to a print which showed the inn as it had been in 1830—a winter day as usual, for the artists in those days were much addicted to snowy scenes—steam rising in clouds from the backs of the horses and coming from their nostrils in jets as from the funnels of the Puffing-Billies that were so soon to replace them. The mail coach had just arrived from London, having taken very little longer over the journey than British Railways take to-day. I can imagine it coming full canter up Elmbury High Street, horseshoes sparking on the cobbles, root-toot-toot on the horn, everybody rushing out of the Swan yard to meet it. I love the air of *busyness* about these old coaching pictures. Things may have been a trifle quiet at the inn betweenwhiles, but when the Mail comes in, what a buzz, what a hum, what a running to and fro of neat little waitresses and stable boys and grooms! The sweating horses are taken out of the shafts, led to the stables, brushed down and the worst of the mud washed off their fetlocks while they are being watered. . . . Crushed oats poured out into the mangers, hay stuffed in the racks, a linseed mash mixed in a bucket if the horses are tired and the night is cold! And meanwhile the fresh horses are harnessed up, restive, well-corned, glossy as cob-nuts; the ostlers bustle about—hostlers as they were then correctly called—green-aproned, shirt-sleeved, tightly-breeked; and the postboys carry out foaming tankards in which the ale or porter is always so much frothier than we see it to-day. The whole sense of the picture is one of warm welcome; what fun, you think, it must have been to arrive at an inn after a long cold journey in 1830. But alas, nowadays the chances are that you will be frigidly received by a sour-faced thin-lipped female more suitable for employment in a Food Office during the strictest period of rationing, she whom they call the Receptionist, though I often think she would be better named a Rejectionist as she snaps out " Have you booked? ", obviously hoping you haven't so that she may have the extreme pleasure of telling you the hotel is full.

BEFORE I leave the Swan bar (and I am finding it as difficult to tear myself away as the Colonel did when he'd had what he called his whack of whisky and was wondering whether he'd exceed it)— before I leave its friendly hearth I must take you round the corner into the " snug " which adjoined it and show you a very different set of pictures from the sporting prints. These old photographs were already faded when I was a young man; you had to switch on the light to see them properly. One, taken after a church parade, showed the local company of Militia in the days before Lord Haldane turned them into Territorials. Very quaint and amateurish they looked, scarcely disguised by their khaki uniforms, family men dressed up as soldiers, only warlike as to their moustaches and even those had the appearance of false moustaches. I used to look at that photograph and smile; but truly they were not to be mocked, for only a few years later they were in France, retreating upon Mons; they and their fellows were all that stood between the Kaiser and his ambition to dominate the world. And flanking this photograph were two small ones, of Elmbury's football team and Elmbury's cricket team in 1913. The footballers wore rather long shorts, and striped jerseys buttoned up tight to the neck; the cricketers wore absurd little caps with very short peaks, and shirts rolled only half-way up the forearm. I thought they looked very funny until one day I noticed some little crosses, subsequently added, against the list of names at the bottom of the photographs. There were eight crosses against the footballers' eleven, seven against the cricketers'.

And those were the Golden Boys of 1913: fifteen crosses out of twenty-two, fifteen graves in France, Salonika, the Dardanelles. . . .

HOW FORTUNATE by comparison were the Volunteer Cavalry of 1814, one hundred years earlier, who were represented in an engraving that hung above the Snug mantelpiece—splendid and fierce upon their shining horses, armed with sabre and musket and lance! For they had entered upon an Engagement, the inscription under the picture proudly records, to " serve for as long as the emergency lasted not more than ten miles from their homes." Napoleon triumphant stood upon the shores of France; but let him dare to cross that narrow sea and march all the way to Elmbury, and the Volunteer Cavalry would show old Boney who was the master!

Having served (but not more than ten miles from their homes) for twelve months or so, and the Duke of Wellington having dealt with Napoleon at Waterloo, these gallant Elmburians marched to the Abbey, where they ceremonially laid up their sabres and their flags, and subsequently during a kind of breaking-up party at the Swan got very drunk and, according to the *Elmbury Intelligencer*, " became involved in unseemly brawling ". Bless 'em all. The flags were hung in the Abbey Chancel, and the moths got at them, so that after a few score years they began to look like the tattered colours of a fighting regiment borne triumphantly on many a stricken field. And one day, as I stood in the Abbey, the Verger walked past me with a party of American girls whom he was showing round. I heard one of the girls say: " And were those flags really carried by the Knights at the Battle of Elmbury in 1471 ? " and the Verger, may Heaven forgive him—well, he did not actually say yes but likewise he did not actually say no. He mumbled something which might equally have meant assent or denial. " Gee," said the girl, " nearly five hundred years old! I sure get a kick out of those old flags." I glanced at the Verger, and he had the grace to avert his eyes.

V

And now, some grey day in November, the great winds begin to blow that bring down from the north what my old Colonel used to call the 'foreign duck', as opposed to the locally-bred ones: the little teal with their shrill short whistle, the widgeon crying like lost souls, the odds-and-sods as he described them, chance wayfarers, golden-eye, shelduck, shovellers, rare pintails, goosander, merganser, smew. The Colonel shot them all impartially, as he would have shot a mermaid or brought down a witch off her broomstick, and he ate them all whether they were accounted edible or not; he held that if a thing was a duck you could eat it, and somehow he masticated the merganser which unwisely flew over his head at dusk (looking a bit like a ragged old witch) as he waited by the river for the first of the white-fronted geese riding upon a storm of early October.

These storms of the late autumn sometimes bring us odds-and-sods which not even the Colonel could have eaten: for the currents of the air have their flotsam and jetsam as the sea's do, and the Colonel, who attracted rare birds to himself as to a magnet, once picked up a dead bittern in his fields and a few days later a moribund little auk. Although he knew the name and the habits of every bird that bred in our district, he could never be bothered to look up in the books, if he had any, these strangers, foreigners as he called them rather on the principle that niggers begin at Calais. So the bittern, to him, was 'a sort of outlandish heron' and the little auk was 'a kind of perishing sea-parrot, if you ask me.' They were duly displayed in the Swan, the bittern dead and the little auk

47

nearly so, for the Colonel had been trying unsuccessfully to feed it on bread and milk. On another occasion he came hobbling into the bar with a sack over his shoulder. It contained a live gannet which he had found sitting exhausted beside the brook which ran through his meadows. It was covered with blood, not its own but the Colonel's, for its sharp beak had drilled a neat hole in his forearm through his coat. Having demonstrated it to his cronies he bore it to the police-station, as if he were giving it in charge for assault and battery, and the next day the Inspector took it by car, in a sack, to the nearest Zoo, where it died.

THIS was to be expected; for the gannets and other sea-birds which are overtaken and blown inland by untimely storms have generally run out of fuel and it is very difficult to persuade them to eat and so restore the supply. Not long ago a whole migration of Leech's Petrels was swept out of its course, and scores of the birds, dead or dying, were picked up in the West Midlands. Three fell in our village and were cosseted by schoolboys, but there was really no hope of saving them. Stray gannets reach us almost every autumn and these are generally reported as ' an albatross ' or ' a cross between a wild goose and a swan '. Last year we had two, which the village schoolmaster tried hard to revive with fish. He even sent his boys down to the river to catch dace and bleak for them; he sacrificed the goldfish which somebody had won at the October Fair; he sent to the fishmonger at Elmbury for pounds of herrings. But it was no good. Each of the gannets weighed 4½ lbs., which James Fisher tells me is the critical weight for exhausted gannets: if they are as light as that they are almost sure to die. Number One did so immediately, putting its head between its wings, burying its long slate-coloured beak in its soft feathers, and expiring with dignity and deliberation. Number Two ate a few herrings but was very choosy and always refused any that had been kept from the night before. It stayed alive for three days, then ate one goldfish, vomited, stood on tiptoe and spread its great wings to their full six feet, became for a moment as a bird of heraldry, and thus theatrically took its leave of the world.

IT STRIKES me as strange that these powerful birds are so often blown out of their courses: for they are better aeronauts, I should think, than the buzzard or the kite or the great golden eagle itself. When they plunge, falling plummet-wise for two or three hundred feet upon a shoal of fish, they go at least as fast as a stooping peregrine; the splash as they enter the water is like the impact of a little bomb. Their nearest breeding-place to Gloucestershire is on Grassholm, off the coast of Wales; but the gannets which accidentally visit us are unlikely to have come from there, and have probably lost their way while on southern migration from Scotland. Oddly enough they do not always arrive in stormy weather. One was picked up dead in our village during a period of autumnal calm. Unlike the others, it was plump and in the pink of condition; it had broken its neck. Surely a migrating gannet would fly too high to collide with power-cables or telegraph-wires; so perhaps it was hit by the wing of an aeroplane, possibly one of those jets which howl through our skies like wild witches in a sabbath nightmare.

I WISH I knew more about sea-birds. We inlanders rarely get a chance to observe them, and the one glorious opportunity I had —when I was at sea during the war—was largely wasted owing to the tiresome whims of my Lords of the Admiralty, who always ordered my ship somewhere else just as I was settling down happily to study fulmars, gannets or puffins. Gulls, of course, were always with us, even during an action they would cry their pitiful lament about the ship: flying close alongside they would turn towards us their bright-eyed, hard-bitten faces, the faces of seafarers all the world over. The petrels too, Mother Carey's chickens, used to follow us far out into the Atlantic, when we were looking for submarines; Mother Carey, by the way, is supposed to be a corruption of *Mater cara*, and indeed the French call these far-flying chickens *Oiseaux de Notre Dame*.

What voyagers, what globe-trotters the sea-birds are, some of which breed in one hemisphere and spend the next six months in the other! I have flown from a carrier in mid-Atlantic, ranging a hundred miles or so about her, and have returned to her with the aid of a gyro-compass, a homing beacon, radar, an observer's skilful plotting, and now and then a bit of sheer luck. But one day, when my ship was 2000 miles from the nearest land, a small bird called a phalarope, not much bigger than an English thrush, plonked down on our flight-deck, remained with us for an hour or two, and then took off in the direction of Greenland. On another occasion I saw a whole flock of these small greyish birds riding on the huge Atlantic rollers, and greatly I envied them, for I was nearly out of fuel, like those exhausted gannets, and my Swordfish would not have floated if I had come down in the sea.

Sometimes when I was flying in formation (which I hated and never found easy) I used to envy the knots. These gregarious waders fly in flocks five or ten thousand strong, and the flocks weave themselves into strange serpentine patterns in the sky. The birds are packed densely, wingtip to wingtip, yet when one turns all turn. There are no collisions, there is no confusion, and in a split second the whole immense cohort has changed direction, often simultaneously in both the vertical and horizontal planes. If the sun happens to be shining you see the light-pattern alter on their wings and as they turn the whole flock blinks a semaphore-flash of white. How do they manage, so many of them, to turn so quickly? By sharper eyesight, I suppose, and swifter-acting reflexes, than we earthbound ones can even imagine.

THE WAY of a bird in the air, which was one of the things too wonderful for the author of the Book of Proverbs, is likewise too wonderful for me. I shall never understand how the Pacific golden plover navigates itself across 2,000 miles of ocean without a single landmark on its route; how the greater shearwater after a trip round the Atlantic by way of Greenland, Iceland and Cape Verde finds its way back to the tiny island of Tristan da Cunha where it breeds. But if an amateur naturalist may make a guess, mine would be that most birds fly by sight and topographical memory; not by instinct or sixth sense. They may *inherit* memories of temperatures and prevailing winds, which would be a kind of instinct. But fog and low cloud always beats them, as it beat airmen before radar was invented. So I think they navigate mainly by visual means—even across the wastes of the ocean. After all, what to me may seem an illimitable forest of undistinguishable trees is to a jungle tracker as full of landmarks as a familiar street. The Western Desert (which Sir Winston Churchill is said to have described as " acres and acres of arid austerity—how Stafford would have loved it! ") is to the Arab's eye criss-crossed with well-marked tracks and divided into clearly-defined areas by the wave-patterns of wind-blown sands. And I flew so much over the sea during the war that I am sympathetic with the theory so well summarised by Mr. W. R. Phillipson in his *Birds of a Valley*: " It is possible that to oceanic birds the sea is no more featureless than a landscape is to us. A bird which lives continuously on the sea may well be sensitive to changes in its salinity or warmth, and look upon its currents as we do upon rivers, and may even distinguish between the plants and animals of its surface layers, as we do between a forest and a desert."

IF YOU have yourself been an aviator, you can get a special interest out of watching birds; you understand some of the complicated problems involved in being airborne which they are conditioned to deal with in the course of their day-to-day affairs. Standing by the river the other evening, waiting for the wild duck, I watched four swans take off on their short evening flight to the pool three miles away where they spend the night. They are clumsy birds, almost as clumsy as those old Walrus aircraft which I flew in the Fleet Air Arm, and are obviously underpowered in relation to their weight. They need a long run for their take-off, and preferably a stiff breeze. They retract their undercarriages as soon as they are airborne, big webbed feet are tucked into the fuselage-feathers, and of course when they are landing they lower their undercarriages and apply the air-brakes in their wings. This quickly slows the steep glide, and they finally touch down with the nose held high, as we used to land our aeroplanes on the carrier.

All birds, of course, land and take off into wind, or at least they should do: but young rooks, doing their early solos, sometimes make the same mistakes which inexperienced pilots make and land crosswind, or hold off too high, stall, and crash. The crash doesn't hurt them much, but it is a blow I think to their self-esteem. They waddle away rather quickly and with an air of pretending that nothing went wrong.

But no birds remain Prunes for long. Very soon they are complete masters of their element, experts in the particular kind of flying for which their build and streamlining best fits them: the humming-bird is a hoverplane, the peregrine and the gannet are dive-bombers, the teal is as manœuvrable as a single-seater fighter at high speed.

SOME BIRDS are aerobatic, notably jackdaws, which seem to perform complicated manœuvres simply for fun—as indeed tumbler pigeons do, and peewits during their evening flight just before dusk. As far as I can see the peewits go in for half-rolls, one to the right, one to the left, executed in rapid succession. The tumbler pigeons put themselves into a kind of spin. But the jackdaws, especially when they are teasing some other bird such as a buzzard, perform correct flick-rolls, stall turns (just in front of the buzzard's beak) and even rolls off the top of a loop. I have never yet seen a bird do a complete loop and suppose it to be impossible; if so this is one up to me. I once for a bet drank a whole pint of beer without spilling more than a few drops of it, holding the tankard in one hand and the joystick in the other, while I pulled an old Moth over in a very tight loop. Let me add that there is no special skill in this; it is something to do with centripetal force; and any pilot can do it if he is prepared to put up with the subsequent attack of hiccups.

I SUPPOSE the most exciting thing, for any airman who watches birds, is the spectacle of a falcon tearing down upon its prey; for here is the fighter-pilot in action, and he obeys exactly the same rules that war taught us—seize the advantage of height, get above your foe, dive to the attack, approach from behind. But even the falcons make mistakes sometimes. I once saw a hen peregrine stoop at a low-flying flock of duck which were crossing a lake not ten feet above the water. The peregrine came down 'like a bat out of hell', as we should have said in the war, struck one of the duck and tore some feathers out of it, but badly misjudged her height above the water, which is easy to do in a dead calm because an airman flying over water can only guess his height in relation to ripples or waves. So the peregrine pulled out of her dive much too late and slapped her breast against the water as she did so with a sound like a sharp crack; it must have hurt her badly, for she staggered and nearly stalled as she began to climb away. The moment before she hit the water I felt myself, for a second, to *be* a falcon; I could imagine the huge effort to pull out of the dive, the strong tug of gravity, the strain on wings and spread-eagled tail, the blackout or grey-out which she must suffer as what pilots call '*g*' began to affect her and the blood drained away from the brain. It may have been the effect of that '*g*' which caused her to stagger as she rose from the water; but she quickly recovered, and soon her wonderful wings had carried her high into the sky again.

I can understand the fascination of falconry, because of the opportunity it provides to watch a hawk hunting at pretty close quarters, but I never want to possess, least of all to tame, one of these wild and lovely and savage birds. To tame such a feral thing must in any case involve exquisite cruelty; but these torments were devised at a time when bear-baiting was regarded as light entertainment and to witness the hanging, drawing and quartering of a criminal was the equivalent of going up for the Cup-Final; so nobody was likely

to worry about the miseries inflicted upon a hawk. In any case
falconry was an important industry. A good hawk was a valuable
commodity; a great lord's falconer was a senior member of
his household staff. The quaint terms used in connexion with the
sport were familiar to everybody and indeed had become common
usage, as we quickly learn when we listen to almost any play by
Shakespeare. How beautifully he used these terms! For instance,
when Othello says of Desdemona:

> *If I do prove her haggard,*
> *Though that her jesses were my dear heart-strings,*
> *I'd whistle her off, and let her down the wind*
> *To prey at fortune.*

or when Juliet from her balcony cries out to the dark garden where
Romeo lurks hidden from her:

> *O for a falc'ner's voice*
> *To lure this tassel-gentle back again!*

But if I possessed a hawk, I know that before long I should
' whistle her off and let her down the wind '—what a heart-lifting
phrase!—for I could never bring myself to confine one. I did, as
a matter of fact, for a few days keep a sparrow-hawk. It had been
injured, possibly by a keeper's shot, and it couldn't fly; I thought
its wing might mend if I looked after it. But it perched implacable
in its improvised cage, refusing all food, and regarding me with
bleak hatred out of the most beautiful eyes in all nature. Then it
drooped; and with horror, all one day, while I tried to tempt it
with morsels, I saw the beauty of those eyes fading, they became
lack-lustrous, a film crept over them, and my only tassel-gentle
—but far from gentle, tameless to the end—made a brief flutter to
the corner of the cage, flopped down, and died there. I know
I couldn't have done anything to save her; she would perhaps have
died sooner in the wild. But I was uncomfortably aware that she
died hating the cage and hating me. I never want to see a sick
hawk again; nor a healthy one save when it has the freedom of the

whole wide sky, when its lovely wings like oar-blades cleave the air, bearing it so swiftly down the wind to prey at fortune.

Down the wind, some night in the neighbourhood of Hallowe'en, come the wild geese which the Colonel loved, the first small V-shaped gaggles on their way to the feeding-grounds called the Dumbles, where Peter Scott has established the Severn Wildfowl Trust as their sanctuary. They are mostly white-fronts, with a few greylags, and generally they pass high overhead and offer few chances to the gunners who go out at dusk or dawn in the marshes and meadows by the river. The Colonel used to wait for them with Sweep at his side, and even in his later days, when he became too deaf to hear the clamour in the sky, he still went goose-shooting and used Sweep as his spotter, for the Labrador had ears keen enough for two. The Colonel would simply watch the dog; and only when Sweep cocked his head and looked up into the sky would he raise his own grizzled head and turn his eyes in the direction in which Sweep's long muzzle was pointing. Then perhaps he would catch a glimpse of the gaggle going over; and if they were in range a glimpse was all he needed, for he was the best shot I have ever known. This curious partnership of dog and man once resulted in a bag of three white-fronts, fetched down out of a stormy night-sky when scuds of black cloud were blowing across the moon.

But most of us do not get a sight of this vanguard of the big goose-flocks which will come later; they are a sound in the sky only, a far faint chatter which grows louder, louder, until it becomes a kind of yelping, as if there were ghostly hounds up there in the wind. A moment later it is gone; but although the yelping is so brief, a matter of seconds only, it is surprising how many people hear it, how many men come into the pub that night with their coat-collars turned up and a boding of winter about them, saying: " The geese be going over. . . . Maybe we'll get some snow. . . ."

VI

MAYBE we'll get some snow.... So now I'll be a willing Caliban, sawing and carrying the big apple-logs which make the merriest of fires. They do not give out as much heat as oak, nor are lit so easily as ash which you can burn green, when it bubbles and hisses and sighs and moans as if you were roasting a heretic there. But apple's flame is pure and bright, and it makes as happy a hearth as anybody could wish for. God forbid that I should ever sit before a gas-fire or warm my toes at an electric one. A hearth should be a real hearth, open for preference, with the logs crackling and the flames shooting this way and that; pictures should form in them as you half-close your eyes—and whoever saw pictures in an electric fire? Grey wood-ash, accumulated for weeks, should make a soft bed for the logs to lie on; later it will go on the garden, and provide some potash for the tomatoes. The dry logs should crackle cheerfully as they burn,—no big bangs of course, but a cannonade as of Lilliputian armies. And before this ideal winter hearth at least two cats should be purring.

OF COURSE, a red setter would look very handsome there; or you may prefer a Dalmatian, that absurd and decorative creature, or a spaniel whose tail, too ready to wag, goes flop-flop on the floor in pathetic gratitude should you happen to mention his name. But for me it must be a cat; and indeed a home without a cat would be as incomplete as if it lacked pictures, or books on the shelves.

Dog-lovers, I suppose, are people who like to 'own' their animals. They are pleased or at any rate they are not embarrassed when that devoted spaniel with its ever-wagging tail turns up to them its brown and docile eyes and seems to say "My Lord, my Master, Creator of my world!" But I don't want to be any creature's god, I hate to be fawned upon, I do not desire that any living thing shall 'spaniel me at heels'. (How Shakespeare hated the servility of spaniels!) You can never own a cat; with her it's a relationship much more subtle and tenuous, founded on mutual respect and mutual good manners. You've got to be polite to a cat. If you shout at your dog it obeys or cringes; if you try shouting at a cat she'll either ignore you or answer you back with the ultimate feline insult, which consists in very deliberately washing behind her ears.

Glancing through Lady Aberconway's most erudite *Dictionary of Catlovers* I tried to discover what kind of people had preferred this kind of relationship with an animal to the possession of a 'pet', which is a word applicable to dogs but quite meaningless as far as cats are concerned. The cat-lovers are curiously assorted. Among the poets are Yeats, Wordsworth, Swinburne, Rossetti, Herrick,

Cowper, Byron and T. S. Eliot: the novelists include Wells, Capek, Sterne, Pater, George Moore, Hardy, Dickens, Scott, Mrs. Humphrey Ward, and of course Compton Mackenzie. Whistler and William Nicholson and Hogarth among the painters; Cardinal Wolsey; Isaac Newton; the naturalist Waterton, and W. H. Hudson (who hated dogs); and Thomas Wainewright, that accomplished poisoner, who administered arsenic in large doses to at least four human beings but would not have hurt a hair of his precious cat. The politicians are represented by Mr. Gladstone (who was painted with a cat sitting on the back of his chair while the Grand Old Man, and from its absorbed expression apparently the tabby too, read Homer's Odyssey in the original Greek) and of course by Sir Winston Churchill, whose marmalade tom called Nelson used to lunch at table with the distinguished guests at Number 10 Downing Street during the war.

But the French provide more cat-lovers than any other nation for this delightful anthology. During the nineteenth century there was hardly an eminent poet in France who did not write at least one piece about cats. Baudelaire, of course, was nearly a cat himself (" a voluptuous wheedling cat with velvety manners ", said Gautier) and in his *Fleurs du Mal* there are three poems in which you can almost hear him purring. The best of the three, in praise of *Les chats puissants et doux*, conjures up in four marvellous lines a sense of the shadows in which cats have half their being:

> *Amis de la science et de la volupté,*
> *Ils cherchent le silence et l'horreur des ténèbres;*
> *L'Erèbe les eut pris pour ses coursiers funèbres,*
> *S'ils pouvaient au servage incliner leur fierté.*

KAREL CAPEK, of all the writers, came nearest to understanding cats. Here is an astonishing passage in which he wrote down what he imagined his cat was thinking about him:

That thing there is My man; I am not afraid of him. He is

very strong, because he eats a lot; he is an All-eater. ('What art thou eating? Give it to Me!') He is not beautiful, for he has no fur. He hasn't enough spittle, so he has to wash himself with water. He purrs hoarsely and much more than he need. Sometimes he purrs in his sleep. (' Open the door for Me! ')

I don't know why he has come to be the Master; perhaps he has eaten something grand. In My rooms he keeps things clean. In his paw he carries a sharp black claw and digs into white leaves with it. He can't play in any other way. He sleeps at night instead of in the day, he can't see in the dark, he has no pleasures. He never thinks about blood, never dreams about hunting and fighting, never sings for love.

Often at night when *I* hear secret and enchanting voices, when I see how everything comes to life in the dark, *he* sits at the table with his head down—always, always scratching at the white leaves with his little black claw. (' Don't imagine I am bothering about *thee*! I am only listening to the quiet scraping of the claw.') Sometimes it is suddenly silent; the poor stupid head can't play any more, and then I get sorry for him, and like to go close, and I purr quietly, in a sweet distressing way, out of tune. Thereupon My man lifts me up and buries his warm face in My fur.

Just then, for an instant, a glimmer of the higher life awakes in him, and he sighs with well-being, and he purrs something one can scarcely understand.

(' But don't suppose I am bothering about *thee*! Thou hast warmed Me up, and now I'll go out again and listen to the dark voices.') ...

It's a beautiful bit of writing, and most closely observed: my own cat, Candy, behaves in exactly the same way when she sits on my desk. She gravely watches the scratching black claw; for a short while it interests her, and then she grows tired of it, wishing I could learn to play in a less boring way. So she draws attention to herself by doing a little devil-dance on the desk, or by rubbing her face against mine, or seizing the top of my fountain-pen between her teeth as if she thought she could make a better job of writing than I can.

CANDY has a lively intelligence which sometimes shows itself as a kind of precognition; she seems to know about certain events before they happen,—e.g. when I am going to catch the early train to London. Most cats, I think, possess this faculty, and of course there is nothing supernatural about it. They simply observe everything that goes on and associate certain small differences in the household routine with the happenings that generally follow them. Since they observe with their ears and their noses as well as with their eyes we do not always understand their processes of deduction. For instance I don't know how Candy knows when it is Sunday. At seven o'clock every Sunday morning she jumps on to the bed, purring loudly; if I don't wake up promptly she tweaks my nose. She is aware that I cook the breakfast on Sunday, out of which she receives certain perks. But how can she tell it *is* Sunday? She can't count the days of the week; and I don't believe in any mysterious ' sixth sense '. So my guess is that something, somewhere, happens *differently* before 7 a.m. on Sunday. Either a farm labourer who on weekdays goes up the lane at 6.30 stays late abed; or my neighbour's farm-tractor doesn't start up at the usual time. Something like that. Anyhow, Candy seems to know it's Sunday and her nose-tweak says: For goodness' sake get up, lazybones, and cook *My* breakfast.

Theodore Roosevelt had a cat called Slippers who absented himself from the White House for days and weeks at a time. "But however long he stayed away, he never failed to turn up just before a big diplomatic dinner. . . . Anyone who kept a steady eye on the White House didn't need to be told by the newspapers when a State Dinner was impending. When he saw Slippers sunning himself on the front steps, that was enough. The invitations were out! "

This diplomatic cat who himself required no invitation card

would march into the State Dining Room calm and self-possessed among the officers in their fine uniforms, the great ladies in their evening dresses, the generals, the admirals, the kings and queens. Once the whim took him to lie down in the doorway just as they were walking in procession out of the dining-room, so that they had to step aside to avoid treading on him; and Mr. Roosevelt, just for fun, bowed to him gravely—whereupon the ambassadors of Great Britain and France and Italy and Germany, of all the Empires and the little kingdoms followed suit, paying their respects to Slippers with stiff and formal diplomatic bows!

OUR OWN cat-establishment consists of Candy, whose senior position is unassailable, a chocolate-box foolish film-star of a cat called Floosie, and Scarlett, who has had 70 kittens. We never drown them; for they have the reputation of being good mousers and the neighbouring farmers book them a litter ahead. I can never understand people who, to save themselves trouble, have female cats 'done'. They miss so much; for the play of half-grown kittens is an exquisite spectacle. It was my friend Moray McLaren who said to me that he couldn't imagine why anybody went to dirt-track riding or greyhound racing or boxing matches when he could sit down and watch a kitten having a game. " If I were a Caliph," said Moray McLaren, " and bored, and all the wealth of Islam at my command, to buy whatever I would that might titillate my satiety, I should not call for new dancing-girls. I should have made for me a little arena, concave, of polished black marble; I should throw into it a white ping-pong ball, and introduce to the ping-pong ball two white kittens, spotless as the snow; and I should lean back on my *diwan* and watch them playing . . ."

Their game, of course, is a kind of soccer; they dribble as skilfully as any inside forward. But that is kitten-play, and later on they go in for more individual games. Cats express their personalities in play; and each cat is as different from other cats as humans are from other humans. They have preferences and dislikes as irrational and curious as ours. There is a cat in the village that is very nearly a vegetarian. He likes cooked beetroot and raw cucumber; and his mother, who was as strict as Shaw and eschewed all meat, had a passion for tomatoes, which she would steal off the table, and for raw peas—she would jump on her mistress's lap when the peas were being shelled and passionately plead for them. Quite a lot of cats fancy asparagus, which like other sensible people they enjoy best if it is dipped in melted butter.

BECAUSE of their personalities, cats name themselves. Samuel Butler, rather foolishly, observed that if he had to set an examination paper to test a person's inventive power and ability as a writer, the only question he'd ask would be: Can you name a kitten? But surely the name cannot come until the little personality is formed —unless it's a literary name: his own cat was called Tybalt. Edward Lear's, on the other hand, was Foss.

> *How pleasant to know Mr. Lear!*
> *Who has written such volumes of stuff!*
> *Some think him ill-tempered and queer,*
> *But a few think him pleasant enough . . .*
>
> *He has many friends, laymen and clerical;*
> *Old Foss is the name of his cat,*
> *His body is perfectly spherical;*
> *He weareth a runcible hat.*

I don't suppose he knew why Foss got himself that name (he lived by the way to be 17 years old) any more than he knew what a runcible hat was.

He drew Foss's picture, showing him as a tiger-striped tabby wearing the rather unpleasant, square-jawed and jowly expression which seems to have been common among cats in the nineteenth century, if we can judge from the contemporary drawings. I imagine that selective breeding, practised in a rough and ready way by their human masters, has already changed the appearance of cats, as it certainly has of dogs, pigs, sheep and cattle. Our domestic animals reflect, even as do our dress and our furniture, the taste of a generation.

Nevertheless there are still a few atavistic old Toms to be met with whose old-fashioned and early Victorian look (they are rather like Mr. Gladstone) reminds me of Edward Lear's portrait of Old Foss; or even of the baleful and glowering Hodge as he is represented in the first illustrated editions of Boswell's *Johnson.*

THIS HODGE, Dr. Johnson's cat, emerges as a rather sinister figure from Boswell's brief references to him. We know that the Doctor used to hobble down to the market place upon his dropsical legs to buy oysters for Hodge, and that he performed this office himself instead of sending his negro servant lest " Francis's delicacy might be hurt, at seeing himself employed for the convenience of a quadruped." Oysters were certainly cheap in those days; but it was not for that reason Dr. Johnson bought them for Hodge. According to Mrs. Piozzi " the creature had grown old and sick, and could eat nothing but oysters." My own theory is that Hodge somewhat tyrannised the Doctor. Boswell, who loathed cats and suffered greatly from the presence of Hodge whenever he visited the Doctor, describes him as " scrambling up Dr. Johnson's breast, apparently with much satisfaction, while my friend, smiling and half-whistling, rubbed down his back, and pulled him by the tail." Boswell, to please the Doctor, then brought himself to admit that Hodge was a fine cat. The Doctor replied " Why, yes, Sir, but I have had cats whom I liked better than this," and then, " as if perceiving Hodge to be out of countenance," added " But he is a very fine cat, a very fine cat indeed."

There was another time when Dr. Johnson, speaking of the despicable state of a young gentleman of good family, said " Sir, when I heard of him last he was running about town, shooting cats." And then he bethought himself of his own favourite cat, and said: " But Hodge shan't be shot: no, no, Hodge shall not be shot."

I have a fancy that on each of those occasions Hodge with his baleful eyes glanced at Dr. Johnson; and that he who feared no man living was a little frightened of Hodge. This puts a rather different complexion upon the oyster-buying, I think Hodge *sent Dr. Johnson for his oysters*. Whatever the relationship between them it is quite clear it wasn't that of " master " and " pet."

INDEED, as I said before, if you like that relationship you must keep a dog; if you want blind devotion and unswerving faithfulness you will keep a dog (for a cat will give you neither, though she will show you true affection whenever she thinks you deserve it!) Likewise if you want a creature that can be taught clever tricks you'll keep a dog. Happily cats will not allow themselves to suffer this indignity, wherefore foolish people declare that cats are less " intelligent " than dogs. I cannot believe that an aptitude for learning tricks is an indication of intelligence; doesn't it simply mean that the creature's reflexes are easily conditioned with the aid of biscuits and bones? I don't know; I'm not a biologist; but I should have thought that the only conclusion one could draw from a dog's ability to sit up and beg with a biscuit on its nose, which it throws in the air and catches at the command " Paid for ", was a somewhat unfavourable conclusion about the intelligence both of the dog and of its owner.

I hate to see animals made ridiculous. One of the things that make me unreasonably angry is the spectacle of a dog dressed up. People who enjoy this joke generally give it a gorblimey cap and balance spectacles upon its nose. A friend of mine who was in Naval Intelligence during the war stuck up a notice in his office which ran:

> " I cannot believe that the publication of pictures of bulldogs wearing sailors' caps, at whatever angle, can be regarded as favourable propaganda for the Royal Navy."

But the pictures continued to appear, and they still came to my friend for censorship, since it was thought that the ships' names on the cap-ribbons might in certain circumstances give information to the enemy.

ANIMALS hate being laughed at. The late E. G. Boulenger, when he worked at the Zoo, told me a terrible story about a chimpanzee. He was a man who loved all the creatures that mankind generally despises, snakes and monkeys for example; I sometimes thought he loved them better than he did the visitors who gaped at them. He held that the monkeys were much more likely to catch fleas from the visitors than vice versa, and that " the purpose of the cages was not so much to protect people from the animals as to protect the animals from people." The chimpanzee story, which he said was true, profoundly moved him.

A zoologist, seeking to demonstrate to some of his friends the remarkable intelligence of the Higher Apes, asked a specially-trained chimpanzee to dinner. This chimp, as the principal guest, sat on his right; and the host arranged that the service should go from left to right so that the monkey could imitate the other guests and take his cue from them as each dish was served.

The soup, the fish, the joint, the sweet and the savoury presented no difficulties to the imitative animal. He used the right knives, forks and spoons in the right way. But when the dessert arrived—it included a large dish of cherries piled high upon the plate—he was moved to commit his only solecism. He adored cherries; and the sight of that great red heap of luscious fruit was too much for him. He jumped up on his chair and clapped his hands. The guests thought that was extremely funny; and they laughed. With the sound of their laughter ringing in his ears, the chimpanzee sat down and covered his face with his hands. Human laughter, that braying sound, must be a terrible noise to an animal; and he knew that the mockery was directed at himself. The contrite guests tried hard to persuade him to eat the bright cherries on which he'd set his heart; but he couldn't be persuaded. He remained until the end of the dinner huddled wretchedly in his chair, with his hands before his face, whimpering.

Of course it was nobody's fault. If the host had been quicker-witted he might have leapt to his feet and clapped too; if the guests had been better-mannered they might perhaps have followed suit and so saved the situation. As it was, they were probably all as miserable (and ashamed) as the chimp himself; for they were accessories, if by accident, to the worst social crime anybody can commit, the awful sin of causing a person—or an animal—to *lose dignity*. It is the crime for which I can never forgive Feste and Maria and Toby Belch, in their baiting of Malvolio; it's the reason why I won't watch performing lions or tigers or even dogs, because when they do their absurd tricks they lose their animal dignity. My fellow humans, it seems to me, who go into fits of laughter at such tricks and split their sides over a poodle dressed up as a sailor dancing a hornpipe—they haven't got any dignity to lose.

So I don't go to circuses, and I don't much like zoos; I have never really liked them since my first visit to Regent's Park, when a kindly F.Z.S. who had some influence with the keepers took me there on a Sunday when I was ten. I was allowed to go into the back premises of the Reptile House, where a big python had just had a meal and so was very sleepy and accommodating. One coil of him was lifted up to my shoulders, and I can remember my surprise and relief that he was warm and dry and rather pleasing to the touch, instead of being cold and slimy. I leaned back and imagined I was Mowgli cushioned in the comfortable armchair that Kaa used to make himself into when he hissed out his ancient tales.

But then we went to see the black panther; and I didn't like that part of the visit at all. In the *Jungle Books*, you remember, Bagheera is ' light, strong and terrible '; and indeed a black panther is one of the half dozen most beautiful creatures that walk upon the earth. A black panther in a cage is correspondingly dreadful to see. If ever a beast was born for freedom it is that great rippling cat.

And of course I remembered that Bagheera himself had been in the King's cages at Oodeypore.

I WAS DELIGHTED when I read the other day that Dr. Konrad Lorenz, surely one of the greatest authorities on animal behaviour, admires the *Jungle Books* not only as works of art but as 'sound natural history.' "If animals could speak, this is how these animals *would* speak."

I was given my *Jungle Books* when I was nine, in exchange for *Peter Pan* which an aunt had presented me for Christmas and of which I had ventured to tell her that it was "sloppy stuff". She exclaimed "You unnatural child!" but after a moment of rather painful silence she added: "I expect the bookshop will change it. Give it back to me." And this I was very willing to do for I had just come to a sentence which ran:

"Every time a child says 'I don't believe in fairies' there is a little fairy somewhere that falls down dead."

I demolished a few dozen fairies with satisfaction before the Aunt returned with the two volumes of the *Jungle Books*. I read them both in a day, leaving out the stories which weren't about Mowgli. That's to say I read how Mowgli was brought for inspection to the Council Rock of the Seeonee wolf-pack—" Look well, look well, O wolves! "—and how Bagheera the black panther bought his life for the price of a bull newly killed; how Baloo the wise old bear taught him the Law of the Jungle; how the monkey-people stole him away, carrying him on a crazy journey through the tree-tops above the jungle, and how Kaa the python came to his rescue; and how he killed Shere Khan, the wicked old lame tiger. And in the second volume I read about the great drought in the jungle, and about Mowgli's visit to the evil white cobra who guarded the king's treasure under the ruined city, and about the deadly battle between the wolf-pack and the red dogs. At the end of that fight, when the old grey wolf Akela was killed, I cried. And in the last story in the book, when Mowgli says good-bye to old blind Baloo and Bagheera and Kaa, I felt as if I was saying good-bye to them too and I was broken-hearted.

Now why, I wonder, did I at the age of nine despise and dis-believe in Barrie's fantasy of *Peter Pan* (I still despise it) and yet believe with all my heart in Kipling's animals-that-talked? I think it was because Kipling's jungle-world, however fantastic, was never-theless a sort of microcosm of the real world which I knew about and was just beginning to understand.

There was Law in it, emphasised with a capital L; and at school, and even in the nursery, we are subject to a sort of Law and a sort of Order. But Peter Pan's and Wendy's world of fairies and wishes existed in sheer defiance of natural order. It was the erratic, pointless and fortuitous nature of that fairy-world which made it difficult even for a child to accept it.

But it was easy to accept the hierarchies of the jungle, with Hathi the elephant ruling like a king and Tabaqui the jackal skulking like a sycophantic hanger-on; because I knew there were kings and hangers-on in real life. It was very easy indeed to believe in the Bandar-log, the foolish chattering monkey-people, because I had seen them running down the streets of my home town, yelling and waving flags, on some occasion of local or national rejoicing.

And of course it was easiest of all to believe in Baloo and Bagheera and Kaa because they possessed nobility. Loyalty, courage, stoicism, honour are qualities which a child quickly recognises; if you want to test this rather extraordinary fact all you have to do is to search your memory and discover what character in history or fiction *you* most admired at the age of ten.

I shall be surprised if that character did not only possess some sort of splendour but also *said* splendid things. Now Kaa, Bagheera, Baloo, Akela represent a true aristocracy; and they speak as nobility should. When Akela raises his terrible scarred head to sing the Death Song after his last fight, Phao the new leader cries to the fleeing Red Dogs, " Howl, dogs! A Wolf has died to-night! "

Kaa the python, 30 feet long, weighing half a ton, says with proud understatement, " I speak for no small people " when he gives to Mowgli the freedom of the middle jungle where the great snakes live. And when Baloo is introducing the Black Panther to Kaa and he begins, " Now Bagheera here——" and obviously means to say something more about him, Bagheera cuts him short. " Bagheera is—Bagheera," said the Black Panther, and his jaws shut with a snap."

YOU CAN imagine then what a shock it was to me, at the age of ten, to see this proud and splendid aristocrat Bagheera pad-padding up and down in a cage. The big cats should have no place in circuses or zoos; they are not tameable. Even the little one, the harmless necessary cat upon the hearth, is not really tame. Candy, with hundreds of generations of hearth-sitters behind her, may be all domesticity for an hour. She rubs against my legs, coaxingly. Then she looks up at me and I see her eyes growing large and yellow and luminescent as she measures the distance between herself and my shoulder. One jump, and she's up there, purring with what Karel Capek called a sweet distressing purr and tickling my face with her whiskers until I go into the larder and give her a reward. But all of a sudden her mood changes. The 'dark voices' call her. Imperiously she demands to be let out. As soon as the door is open she runs through it swiftly and her black shape melts into the shadows,—

> *Cats, no less liquid than their shadows,*
> *Offer no angles to the wind.*

Already she has cast aside her domesticity and put on her sinuous swift wild *alter ego* without even bothering to wish me good-bye. No tail-wagging thank-yous from her; she's off on her own dark business under the moon; she will not think of me at all while she's hunting, nor would I have it otherwise, for I do not want to possess her.

But the black panther padding and padding, inside the bars, up to the trap-door, back to the bars, back to the trap-door—when he hears the dark forest voices, cry they ever so loud to him, cry they till his heart breaks, nobody will open the door and let *him* out. Nobody, ever.

"No LESS liquid than their shadows." The poem is by A. J. S. Tessimond; it goes on:

> *They slip, diminished, neat, through loopholes*
> *Less than themselves,*

And indeed I am sure that their personalities are as elusive as their bodies, they are unpossessable, you have them and yet you have them not.

There was one, a little Siamese we called Mishy, whom we came near to possessing, and then she slipped out of our lives as through a chink in a door. She was so very small, a fairy-cat almost, who would dance the steps of ballet dances to herself daintily, and whose strange conceit it was to steal hair-curlers and pipe-cleaners, which she would carry about in her mouth, and hide in secret places, and curiously cherish.

But apart from this quaint fancy, she was a sedate cat, and very gentle, and her paws were always soft in play. She rarely cried or called as other Siamese do—even in courtship she was silent, and when she had kittens it was always a surprise to us, and I think a surprise to her, too. They were always black kittens and, by Siamese standards, illegitimate; but all were very small and somehow fairy-cats like herself.

She was only once demonstrative. We came back to the house after a fortnight abroad and all that day, all the next, all the next week, she was our faithful shadow. She didn't talk the loud hectoring Siamese-talk, she just trotted round, at our heels, softly purring.

That was the time when, as I said, we nearly possessed her. She was in kitten again and as she trotted after us we noticed that she seemed out of breath. We put it down to the kittens. But next day it was clear that her heart was working overtime and she would lie down most of the time, now and then raising her flat head in the hopeless quest for air. That night she began to make dreadful small choking noises, and next day the vet. said " No hope," and gave her the last anæsthetic.

I said she was gentle, and so she was at all times save when she had kittens and there were dogs about. Then she became a spitting fury and her tail fluffed out into a witch's broom. During her illness, that long last fight for her kittens, her tail had been fluffed out all the time.

This happened a year ago, or I could not write about it now. " Brothers and sisters, I bid you beware, Of giving your heart to a dog to tear." Or a cat, or any small dependent creature.

About two thousand years ago the girl called Lesbia wept some salt tears because her little cage-bird had died; and Catullus wrote her plaint in Latin verse of such a singular and moving beauty that it has long outlived him and his Lesbia and her sparrow. Curse upon you, he cried, you cursed shades of Orcus, that devour all pretty things.

So when Mishy died I wrote those lines in my diary and added an epitaph for her from another Roman poet, Martial, an epitaph which seemed just right for her because she was so small, so airy-light, so softly-treading:

> *Mollia non rigidus caespes tegat ossa nec illi,*
> *Terra, gravis fueris; non fuit illa tibi,—*

that is to say

> And let not hard clods cover her tender bones, nor be thou heavy upon her, O earth; she was not so to thee!

> THEY SLIP, *diminished, neat, through loopholes*
> *Less than themselves, will not be pinned*
> *To rules or routes for journeys; counter-*
> *Attack with non-resistance; twist*
> *Enticing through the curving fingers*
> *And leave an angered empty fist.*

And it was just like that, as I say, when Mishy slipped out of our lives into the shadows. How foolish we are, foolish as poor Lesbia two thousand years ago, to give our love to these small unpossessable things!

For always when they go from us, out through the chink in that door through which there is no returning, we are forced against our will to recognise: There can never be *another*. Never another just like that.

There will be loved ones again, but not with precisely those quaint ways, that particular make-up of personality. There are no exact replacements, no duplicates in life's store. Only insensitive people, surely, can return from that job of digging at the bottom of the garden, and put away the spade, and go straight to the animal shop to buy another.

VII

AND NOW the first Christmas cards are on the mantelpiece, not only the arty ones from the people who hold representational robins in contempt, but the stage-coaches and the yule-logs and the old-world cottages iced with snow. Christmas wouldn't be quite Christmas without its vulgarities: *Good King Wenceslas* made up by J. M. Neal in 1855 and now sung at the front door by nice little children with horrid little voices; the bauble-decorated spruce brought to England by Albert the Good ('who also introduced Fish Knives'); a sentimentalised saint from Germany, a turkey from the Americas, a kiss under the mistletoe which solemn folk-lorists derive from the Druidical sacrifice of virgins, and an indigestible pudding which only a heavy-handed English cook could have devised!

We must have the lot; *and* the biggest mistletoe-bough in the whole orchard, which generally grows at the top of the tallest apple-tree, so that I shall need the 40-rung ladder to cut it down. Striving in vain to hold this ladder upright as I carry it towards the tree, I feel like a sea-lion balancing a walking-stick on the end of its nose. Then comes the holly-gathering and the last-minute decorating (for unaccountably the seasons creeping upon us always take us by surprise). But at last we're ready; and it's Christmas Day.

THERE's a kind of nadir between tea and dinner on Christmas Day, when time inexplicably ceases, and clocks tick without meaning, and somehow nothing is quite real. Everybody experiences this phenomenon, nobody can explain it. But it is curiously enjoyable.

Pickwick is the book to read then; or one can tell ghost-stories. The best Christmas ghost of all appeared not twenty miles from my home. "Anno 1670," wrote John Aubrey, "not far from Cyrencester, was an Apparition. Being demanded whether a good spirit or bad? it returned no answer, but disappeared with a curious Perfume, and a most melodious Twang. Mr. W. Lillie believes it was a Fairy."

Pickwick or ghost-stories, no matter which; we shall yawn contentedly and Candy will sit prim and yawning before the fire, forgetting how last night under the wild moon she was compounded of tiger, witch and devil nor apprehending that in a few hours she will be so again. It is a time for smugness, of which we all possess our share. The wind should therefore howl loudly in the chimney. Let it blow its cheeks out, let it twang like Mr. Lillie's melodious apparition, our walls are thick! . . . And just before six o'clock, when we switch on the wireless to hear the news, there should be gale warnings, and the level voice of the announcer should speak to us the names of the sea-areas bluff and salt-sounding, pandering to our smugness and the sense of security engendered by thick walls. Lundy, Dogger, Cromarty, Humber, Heligoland; perhaps if I hadn't spent some war-time Christmases bucketing round about them I shouldn't dare to feel so smug! But they are poetry however you string them together, you can hear the surge of the sea and the roar of the wind in them. So while the wind is loud in the chimney and the great words are still blustering through my mind I try to match some verses to my mood:

> Draw close the curtains. (Mares' Tails streaking the night sky
> And looks like rain?)
> With the wireless going, you won't notice the creeper
> Rat-tatting on the pane.
> Shut out the night with its wild whispering voices,
> Its cries and its calls,
> The tempestuous world kept at bay with your solid
> Inviolate walls.

The Backend of the Year

So settle down to a peaceful finish to Christmas.
               Kick off your shoes;
Cherry-logs merrily crackling, a drink at your elbow,
               Time for the News.
Cat on the hearth, book on your lap, and suddenly over the air,
           Out of the void, into your quiet,
             Come the great sea-names that roar and riot,
Humber, Lundy, Faroes, Forties, Fastnet, Forth and Finisterre!

Tendril of creeper beats a tattoo on the window
               Like a limed linnet.
Know now that you live on an island!—Your house is
               An island within it!
The pitiless winds of the world all about you; and surging
               Into your room
Comes the heave and the sigh and the crash of the steep Atlantic,
               The spray and the spume.
The fire leaps high, and harshly the dry logs sputter.
               The wind has risen!
The chimney always smokes when it's in that quarter. . . .
               Islander, listen:
As the cat gets up and your book falls shut, and suddenly over
                        the air,
           Out of the void, into your quiet,
             Come the great sea-names that roar and riot,
Humber, Lundy, Faroes, Forties, Fastnet, Forth and Finisterre!

Part Two

THE
HUNGRY MONTHS

I

MY OLD COLONEL'S ' arse-end ' finished with Twelfth Night:
finished, for him, in a blaze of glory, since he permitted
himself a dispensation between December 21st, the shortest day,
and January 6th, when the Christmas decorations were taken down.
During this period he need not ration himself to his ' whack ' of
whisky, but could indulge in unlimited whacks, to which he super-
added—of all strange drinks on top of whisky—two large Brown
Sherries each night and morning before he set off home from the
Swan.

But always, by Twelfth Night, he sobered down. He had a
powerful sense of the seasonal fitness of things. The ' hungry
months ' lay ahead: January, February, March, which are nature's
fast times. He who was closer to nature than any man I have
known fasted likewise. He went home early from the Swan
and sat by his fire, reading the only printed pages he ever did read
—the *Compleat Angler* and the Bible on Sundays, seedsmen's catalogues, wine-merchants' price lists, and the obituary notices of old
acquaintances in *The Times*.

TWELFTH NIGHT or Epiphany used to be a general holiday and the
occasion of much merrymaking. The loveliest comedy ever written,
I suppose, was written specially for this occasion, and Feste sang,
Sir Toby belched, Sir Andrew danced his foolish jigs and Maria
bubbled with impish laughter, in king's palace and lord's manor
on the twelfth night after Christmas.

But in the cider country which lies to the west of where I live,
up to a century ago, the evening was dedicated to a very strange

and ancient ritual connected with the spirit of the apple-trees. The men and women would go out into the orchards after dark carrying buckets of cider, shotguns and lanterns. Each in turn would dip a cup into the pail, drink a sip, and pour the rest as a sort of libation over the roots of the trees. They would also dip pieces of cake in the cider and place them in the branches " for the robins to peck at ". Then they sang a merry little song to wassail the trees:

> *I hope your trees will bear and bow*
> *Apples and pears and plums I do vow,*
> *Hats full, cups full, three bushel bags full,*
> *All under the trees, hooray, hooray!*
> (And a little heap under the stairs.)

Finally, to make sure that the Spirit of the Trees, the secret sap in root and branch, was properly wakened they would all let off their guns and pepper the bare twigs, shouting and hollering meanwhile.

I LIKE the notion of putting the titbits of cake in the twigs for the robins. Nowadays, when we pick our apples, we still leave a few on the topmost twigs " for the birds,"—though the starlings and the blackbirds are the ones which generally get the benefit. Robin is not a fruit-eater. He loves to hop about within a few feet of me while I am digging, waiting for me to turn up a juicy grub or a wriggling red worm. He is without fear even of Candy, who also attends me when I am working in the garden; and she seems to know that he is under my protection, or in some way sacred, for she never attempts to catch him. Not that she'd have much luck if she tried!—for his little beady eyes, so bright and lively, are watching her all the time. I have never yet seen a cat with a robin in its mouth; I hope I never shall.

WHAT a foolish superstition it is, that if a robin comes into your house somebody is going to die shortly! I should be only too delighted to welcome the little redbreast; though in fact he never comes any farther than the back door-step. People have odd superstitions about owls too, and sometimes are quite alarmed when they hoot repeatedly just outside their bedroom window. Two or three years ago, however, a tawny owl actually spent the night in our bedroom. The weather was very cold, and I shut the window before we went to bed, unaware that the owl was inside. He remained quiet and unobserved all night and when we woke up in the morning he was sitting on the rail at the bottom of the bed, regarding us with those sad Semitic features, like "a feathered Dreyfus" as W. H. Hudson said, and thinking no doubt what strange slumbering monsters we were. He seemed to be quite without fear of us, and when I opened the window for him he flew out unconcernedly. Some idiot to whom I told this story said: "But weren't you frightened something was going to *happen* to you afterwards?" We felt, instead, that we had been privileged to have such a guest, as I always feel when some wild thing does not fear me unduly and demonstrates, however briefly, its faith that *Homo sapiens* is not such a brute and a blackguard as his treatment of his fellow-creatures often seems to suggest!

II

WHAT a little thing can set the memory running back like a mole through dark tunnels, winding and wending back into the past! This morning in a sharp nip of frost I saw the hot muckheap at the bottom of the garden smoking like an autumn squitch-fire as it always does in the cold, and I saw a thrush that looked as fat as a bantam because of her fluffed-out feathers, and there came into my mind a poet's phrase:

The puffed birds hopping and hunting.

I went back into the house and took down a book and read a wintry tale:

The dunghills white as wool and the hen
Roosts sleeping chill till the flame of the cockcrow
Combs through the mantled yards and the morning men
Stumble out with their spades,
The cattle stirring, the mousing cat stepping shy,
The puffed birds hopping and hunting. . . .

Back burrowed this mole of memory through the honeycombed mind until it emerged at last in a place very far from my frost-furred lawn with its puffed-out thrush, and at a time longer ago than I cared to calculate. The place was a pub, the smoky bar of a pub in Windmill Street, off Tottenham Court Road. The time was perhaps 25 years ago. There was a horrible Pianola churning out a horrible tune; one never saw anybody put any money into it but doubtless somebody did, either because they liked the noise or because they feared the silence. The company was oddly mixed.

There were some pick-pockets and minor criminals and some tarts off the streets; there were some bearded young men who hoped to be painters; there was a dilapidated drunk who would draw your portrait for the price of a double whisky; there were some girls and boys from the Slade School and from the Royal Academy of Dramatic Art who imagined they were seeing Life. There was also, sitting in a corner, a chubby pale-faced youth with a perpetual cigarette dangling from his lower lip, but whose expression otherwise was one of a surprised innocence. He and I fell talking, and we drank a great deal of beer, and later we walked through still streets singing, both being boisterously happy and foolish and young. At last we parted and I went home not knowing that I had met a poet.

In later years we met quite often; and then of course I knew him for what he was, though he still looked the same save that he grew chubbier and if possible a little grubbier, with the ash from the dangling cigarette always smearing his tie and the lapel of his coat. He still had that air of a surprised boy, dumbfounded by the bright-shining, many-faceted, many-coloured world. And when in his poetry he remembered his youth, it was always with that sense of wonder and surprise:

> *And as I was green and carefree, famous among the barns*
> *About the happy yard and singing as the farm was home,*
> *In the sun that is young once only,*
> *Time let me play and be*
> *Golden in the mercy of his means,*
> *And green and golden I was huntsman and herdsman, the calves*
> *Sang to my horn, the foxes on the hills barked clear and cold,*
> *And the sabbath rang slowly*
> *In the pebbles of the holy streams.*

Now the thought that troubles me is, should I have known, should I have realised when I met for the first time the grubby youth in the grubby bar, whose unknown name was Dylan Thomas, should

I have guessed? Surely we ought to recognise poets. We should be aware of haloes about them. They should bear some mark or stigmata upon them. At least as soon as they speak to us we should know! But I didn't know; and we drank our beer together, Dylan and I, and then we strode along Charlotte Street, singing our naughty songs, and talking I dare say of girls and foolishness, and never a word of puffed birds hunting and hopping or the foxes on the hill barking clear and cold.

To-day I read his poems with bitter sadness, because there will be no more of them. And then I read his note at the beginning of the book, written in November, 1952, and sadness vanished and I laughed aloud, for it was as if I heard his own voice speaking:

" These poems, with all their crudities, doubts and confusions, are written for the love of Man and in praise of God, and I'd be a damn' fool if they weren't."

III

THE COLONEL, I told you, read seedsmen's catalogues and wine merchants' price lists during the winter of his discontent. I had another old friend who found himself ill-at-ease in the climate of modern literature, to whom Dylan Thomas's poetry was incomprehensible, and who held that the vintners and the florists were the only real poets left. To the Colonel all poetry was anathema—Bah he'd say, *The lambkin, the lambkin, Riding in its pramkin!* Poetry! Rot!—but perhaps he found a substitute in the names of the hocks and the burgundies—*Liebfraumilch Madonna, Nuits Saint Georges, Château Domaine de Chevalier*—or in the descriptions of daffodils, tulips, and irises. For my part I am hardly to be trusted with a bulb-catalogue. The Dutch ones, which affect an endearing ignorance of the English language and by running two or three words together achieve a kind of crazy Jabberwocky style, are the most seductive of all, and induce me to write cheques which turn my Bank Manager's hair grey.

I SUPPOSE if I have one really appalling extravagance it is in this matter of bulbs. I love their names, Fireglow, Queen of the Pinks, King of the Blues, Gay Hussar. I love ordering them, unpacking them, handling them and planting them; and I generally forget where last year's were planted, so that I mix tulips and daffodils, hyacinths and anemones, in patterns as haphazard as a kaleidoscope's. Irises tempt me most, and are generally the most expensive. Who could resist

" Standards and falls all a similar shade of soft shell-pink, the falls being shadowed with grey when first unfolding. The haft is a much warmer tone, and this is enhanced by the rich tangerine-red beard. . . ."

This is indeed poetry; but it is poetry at 25/– a time.

Anemones are cheap though, and one can buy a big double handful of the little brown withered corms of *blanda* and *appenina* for a few shillings, enough to turn a whole rockery blue as the Mediterranean. And grape-hyacinths are cheap too, and so are scillas and the delicate *Chionodoxa luciliae*, the Glory of the Snow. You can buy enough crocuses to make you believe it's spring when it's still early March for five bob. But alas, the irises tempt me still—

" Large flowers polka-dotted and edged with pure clear blue on a clean, crisp white background . . ."

One guinea!

EVEN the catalogues of vegetable seeds are poetic in a way. I sit down on a January day to make out my annual order; I start with the peas and as I open the catalogue I am faced with a studio portrait of well-filled pods, so well-filled indeed that one has burst open of its own accord to show the peas inside it, as level and regular as a row of National Health teeth. . . . This particular sort is called *Kelvedon Wonder*. There is also *Phenomenon* and there is also *Little Marvel*. Surprise at their own success seems frequent among pea-growers; for there is an *English Wonder* and an *American Wonder* too! It is difficult to choose between all these astonishments; but the Kelvedon is an old favourite that suits my soil.

I pass on to the Broad Beans. One sort has a very pretty name, *Aquadulse*, which makes me think of sweet flowing streams rather than beans; so I choose it in preference to the other kind, *Windsor*. Windsor is associated in my mind with dull and austere things: Brown Windsor soup, and hard Windsor chairs. Did Queen

Victoria sip that soup and immortalise it? Did she seat her Imperial Majesty upon those chairs? I doubt it.

More pictures—this time of Runner Beans 12 inches long. Who wants to eat such monsters? Not I. We shall go in for Dwarf, French Beans, which are steamed whole, tied in little bundles, having first been topped and tailed. But there is much prejudice against them among the muckers-up of good food that pass for cooks in England. They like their beans chopped up like chaff, boiled, butterless, a sort of leguminous spinach. Thus the majority of hotels serve them; and since none of us nowadays has the guts to pick up the dish and chuck the contents at the head waiter à la Charlie-Chaplin-custard-pie, we get what we deserve.

Broccoli next, which we in the Evesham vale call Broccolo, making it somehow sound fierce and hornèd. It bears names such as Snowball and Purity. The pictures of the white foamy soap-suddy heads look like advertisements for detergents. Perhaps the manufacturers of detergents when they have exhausted every name suggestive of the seaside will call a new product Broc. But the heads of my Broccoli never look like these pictures in the catalogue. They are not white, but dirty-yellow, with nasty inexplicable brown stains. They are full of little caterpillars to which even I, a bug-hunter, am unable to give a name.

Summer and autumn cabbage proudly calls itself Drumhead; spring cabbage, on the other hand (which of course doesn't ' heart up ' like the other kinds) bears the sweet name Tender and True, more fitting I should have thought for Juliet, for Ariadne, for Thisbe than for a mere Brassica.

Poetry, you see, is beginning to creep into the catalogue; and already I am ordering wildly, buying twice as many packets as I need. French Breakfast radish (photographed in colour, crimson and white, so crisp-looking you could almost nibble the picture), Silver-skin onion, peeling as coyly as a strip-tease dancer, Scarlet Horn carrot, and so on. By the time I come to the lettuces, Arctic King and May Queen, I am in a mood for versifying myself. Here is a theme, surely, for Swinburne. Do you remember

Come Rain, Come Shine

If you were April's lady
And I were lord in May?

Well, here goes:

If I were King of Arctic
And you were Queen of May,
You'd melt my heart, dear lettuce,
Though it with dewdrops wet is,
If I were King of Arctic
And you were Queen of May.

Can I go on? Indeed I can. So could Swinburne, and he hadn't the advantage of a Florists' catalogue in which most of the poetry is written for one already:

Your little golden buttons,
Your tight hearts meet for gluttons,
Hurray for Messrs. Suttons,
My Lettuce-Queen of May!

You SHOULD never omit from your seedsman's order, if you have any children between five and eight, at least one packet each of mustard and cress. You should then, in February for preference, provide each of the children with a saucer and a small square of flannel... The flannel should be laid in the saucers and allowed to soak up as much warm water as it will. The seed should be sprinkled on the flannel, the cress first, the mustard two days later, because the cress takes a little longer to germinate. In due course a sort of grey fluff will appear upon the seeds. Then they will ' chit '—a tiny shoot sprouting from each. Within a few days there will be green leaves, lengthening stalks: a week later, if your room is a warm one, the children can eat mustard-and-cress sandwiches. Possibly the mustard and cress won't be so good as it would be if you grew it in earth, in a box or pan; but it'll taste fine to the children. The presence of soil would detract from the miracle; even five-year-olds *expect* things to grow in the earth. With the flannel only, they can get a better view of the chits lengthening and the little fibrous roots forming. How does the stuff grow without any ' food ' ?—I suppose it has stored up enough food within the seed to last it at any rate for a fortnight. But *that's* not the miracle. The miracle is germination, life itself.

Now although your children watch television, go to the cinema, read about space-ships and so on without showing the least surprise that these concepts should be, it is nevertheless important that they should know Wonder. And if they can experience Wonder when they watch the seeds growing, there's no great harm in their accepting television as an everyday happening, something you get in return for a three pound licence, the citizen's ' right '. You will probably find it impossible to teach them the wonder of television; for that belongs to your generation and mine. But unless they can know some Wonder, they will lack humility; and the eternal, un-changing, ever-present Wonder is this mystery of Life.

It is the completely fundamental mystery. That man's ingenuity should harness electricity, invent the internal combustion engine, build aeroplanes to fly at 700 m.p.h., and ultimately drive rockets to the stars, is not particularly wonderful once you have accepted the inventiveness and the questing spirit of man. But the wonder is that men exist; and still more that some five hundred million years ago a fusion or combination or creation of matter (have it which way you like) produced by accident or design a tiny cell which grew—which grew as the mustard and cress grows, and pro-liferated, and as it adapted itself to changing conditions itself changed, sprouted organs, legs, eyes, shells, intestines, lungs, tails—giving birth in time to an infinite variety of living creatures ' multi-plex of wing and eye ' which by a process of adaptation and inter-necine warfare, living upon each other, resulted ultimately in fishes, great lizards, birds, mammals, apes, ourselves.

All this from the germ; and although we can transmit sound and pictures by a kind of magic from a studio in London to a cottage in the Cotswolds, although we can transport ourselves from London to New York in a few hours, although we can set off a process of nuclear fission or fusion by which it may be possible to destroy all life upon the earth, WE STILL DON'T KNOW WHAT LIFE IS.

That's why I recommend the mustard and cress as an introduction to humility; without which your children will grow up into the kind of adults you would not wish to contemplate. If they wonder when the seed sprouts, it's enough; for this is the wonder that makes all else commonplace. It even makes the existence of Martians and Venusians a matter for no surprise. After all, if the process started here, it probably started there too; but the climatic conditions being so different, the living organisms probably had to be different in order to adapt themselves to it. And so if a little green man with antennæ like a butterfly's, or a thinking vegetable, a Triffid, appears one morning at my back door, I shall not be really astonished. Why should I be? I experienced the true astonishment forty years ago, when I grew the mustard and cress on the flannel.

ANOTHER rich source of wonder, for me, was my first microscope. It cost about half as much as you would pay nowadays for a small model jet fighter which won't fly, or for a box of lead soldiers. Yet it was much more than a toy. It showed me the shapes of the scales from a butterfly's wing and enabled me to demonstrate to my father the crawling mites in his Stilton cheese. It turned a mosquito into a Dracula and a drop of water from a dirty pond into an aquarium full of animalcules. I doubt if you can obtain these simple, child's microscopes to-day; if so it is a pity, for it is a good thing for the young to have a glimpse of this weird Other-world, pullulating with beauty and horror, that lies beyond our ordinary vision; it is good for their sense of proportion. Parasites, for example, of the kind which fill us with dismay—fleas, lice, flukes and so on—turn out under magnification to be beautiful as well as strange. The appearance of some is as fantastic as their life-histories, which Miss Miriam Rothschild described as "Odysseys beside which Ulysses' journeys sound almost commonplace,"—for one fluke in order to complete its life-cycle has to pass through no less than three different hosts, one which swims on the water, one which lives on the land, one which flies through the air. Other kinds are so specific that in order to survive they must not only find the right kind of host but make their way through its bloodstream to the right part of it—the bile-duct of a chicken, the tentacle of a snail. Tapeworms parasitic in larger animals have parasites which in turn feed on them, and so on; in fact the whole organic world is a complex of creatures mutually interdependent, living upon each other. What is at first pretty horrifying to most of us is the realisation that Man is a link in this endless chain. He who writes a *Hamlet* or designs a Westminster Abbey is no more exempt than any other organism from playing the host in this remarkable relationship. He shares his own particular flea with the pig, his louse with the rat!

BUT I shall never forget my wonder when I first saw that flea on a slide in my toy microscope; nor my first view of the cheese-mites and butterfly-scales and the stamens of a flower. If *I* wondered, at the age of eleven, what of the first man who looked through a magnifying lens at a drop of stagnant water and saw devils swimming there, Lucifer and all his legions, a thousand Beelzebubs reproducing themselves in every cupful, all hell's angels *ingens et horribile, mirabile dictu* inhabiting each bucket of drinking water drawn from the domestic well! It must have been an appalling revelation; but who first received it we do not know unless he were indeed a monk who showed the monsters to Friar Bacon, as Kipling supposes in his short story. This monk, illuminating a manuscript, had drawn in the margin some devils more terrible, than any which had been imagined before, and being invited to explain so vivid a vision of the Pit had shown Roger Bacon his magnifying-glass.

So with my child's microscope did I see devils at the age of eleven; but the manufacturers had obligingly provided me with a little booklet explaining what they were; as indeed we comfortably explain away all devils, in these rational times.

IV

IN A DRY spell during February, which is unjustly called fill-dyke
—it is one of the least rainy months, according to the statisticians—
I saw the sparrows bathering upon the crumbling earth in one of
the flower-beds. Bathering: having a dust-bath. It was one of the
Colonel's words. The old Gloucestershire expressions were always
on his tongue. I've told you how he delighted in the word ' oontitoomps '. Likewise he'd say he was shrammed with the cold on
a bitter day when it was mizzling with rain, or he felt nesh—tender,
delicate, like a greenhouse plant put out too early—when he got
out of a warm bed and pottered about his farm before breakfast.
If he was tired out after a day's haymaking he'd say he was ' fair
forswunk ', forswunk being a kind of past participle of Chaucer's
' swinke ', meaning to work hard. He'd call an overdressed woman
a doxy (and I'd wonder if the word had any association with
Shakespeare's daffodils, Heigh! the doxy, over the dale). If he'd had
to replace a couple of gate-posts—which, lapsing into Gloucestershire, he'd call gee-ut-posses—he'd say " They were all daddocky,
you could cut 'em like cheese." It's a curious word, daddocky,
which we use as an adjective for decaying wood such as you find
at the heart of a dying tree. It means soft and rotten; though
not of fruit, which in such a condition we should describe as
' mawsy '.

   Word-collecting is fun, and it is surprising how often you
come across specimens which even the Oxford English Dictionary
knows nothing of. My best bag was four words that were new to
me, all collected in a village pub in the course of an hour's talk.

These were: puggle, huggle, moff, badikins. The landlord of the pub gave me puggle. He complained that he'd been pretty puggled the night before; and I was delighted to add it to my enormous collection of words meaning ' drunk ' of which there are 73 in Roget's *Thesaurus*, 1925 edition—at least a score, including the delightful ' pixolated ', must have been added since.

But I did not at first know where ' puggle ' came from. Apparently " pagl ' in Urdu means mad or crazy, so it's easy to see how our soldiers in India gave it the connotation of ' drunk '; thus ' puggle ' turns out to be one of the many lively words brought home by Tommy Atkins.

' Huggle ' came up in the course of a conversation initiated by a nasty old man who objected to the Goings-on of Young People Nowadays. " Every blessed night," he said, " when I turns out the cat, there they be, a-hugglin' on my doorstep." Shortly after this conversation I happened to read a late sixteenth century account of the Rogues, Vagabonds and ' Sturdy Beggars ' who at that time were terrorising the countryside; and in it I encountered ' huggle ' again. The author of the account pointed out with righteous indignation that the Sturdy Beggars were sometimes accompanied by girl-friends. Scandalised, he declared:

" So long as he hath his pretty pussie to huggle withal, that is the only thing he desireth."

The dictionaries I have consulted have a lot to say about ' hug ' but nothing about ' huggle '. Nor have they ever heard of badikins, which are part of the arrangement for harnessing a horse to the plough. Actually this contrivance, a cross-bar to which the traces are attached, is variously called within a few miles of my own home badikins, suppletrees, swiveltrees and whippletrees, and a man told me he could guess which village a person came from, by whichever of these words he used.

A moff is a sort of wagon convertible into a cart by the addition of side-boards. I was rather proud of myself for guessing its origin.

" Hermaphrodite! " I said.

" Hermaphrodite," its user corrected me. " Serves two pur-
poses, see."

Sailors of course have always used Hermaphrodite for a dual-
purpose thing; and Kipling called his Royal Marine ' a kind of a
giddy hermaphrodite'; but I had never heard the word used by
inlanders before.

It is surprising how many of our older countrymen, who left
school at twelve or fourteen, seem to love words for their own
sake, regarding them not simply as utilitarian things but as the
decorations of speech, almost as poets do. Their vocabulary is
larger than one would expect; they search in their memories for
some old vivid phrase of their grandfather's and use it to heighten
the effect when they are telling you a tale. But when they write
a letter, they become stilted and conventional, striving to be
' correct'; they hardly ever use the old words then, and perhaps
they would not know how to spell them.

They have probably never seen some of the local field names
spelt; for these are passed on from generation to generation by
word of mouth, and are hardly ever written down save on the farm-
map, or in the deeds in a solicitor's office. I once met a man in a
train who was genuinely astonished to learn that individual fields
had names. He'd been staring out of the carriage window for half
an hour or more, vaguely aware of fields of all shapes and sizes,
square, oblong, oval, pentagonal, some pastured by cows, some
planted with winter corn, some ploughed and lying fallow until the
spring. He could hardly believe it when I told him that every one
of those enclosures bore a name known not only to its owner but
to the men who worked in it and such other countrymen as had
reason to walk over it.

" What sort of names? " he asked me.

I told him a few: Cuckoo Pen, Fiddler's Folly, Cold Elm, The
Forty Acre, Puppy's Playground, Breaking Stone Meadow,
Whistling Down Hay, Mog Ditch, Parson's Piece, Long Furlong....
How they sing to us, these ancient and beautiful names by which

our grandfathers and our great-grandfathers recognised footpath and landmark! The poet Edward Thomas put some of them in a verse:

> *If ever I should by chance grow rich*
> *I'd buy Codham, Cockridden and Childerditch,*
> *Roses, Pyrgo and Lapwater,*
> *And let them all to my elder daughter. . . .*

And again:

> *If I were to own this countryside*
> *As far as a man in a day could ride,*
> *And the Tyes were mine for giving or letting,—*
> *Wingle Tye, and Margaretting*
> *Tye,—and Skreens, Gooshays, and Cockerells,*
> *Shellow, Rochetts, Bandish and Pickerells,*
> *Martins, Lambkins, and Lillyputs. . . .*

Indeed if I were a farmer how proud I should be to own such a domain! Most farmers do. On the big ordnance map hanging on the wall of the back room which they quaintly call their " office " the boundaries of each field are shown, with the name inked in, and sometimes the area: ' Tom Taplow's Hollow 6a 3r 4p.' Who was Tom Taplow? Nobody knows, though you might find out if you chiselled away the moss from one of the tombstones in the churchyard.

Some of the names are poetic, some are obscure, some are funny, though this may be by accident: Betty's Bottom is a field in a hollow which Betty once owned. Quite a few are grim,— Dead Man's Acre, Gibbet Hill, Hangman's Hill, the Murder Piece, and so on. The quaintest and the most pleasing of all are to be found I think in Herefordshire. All the place-names there are delightful; and whenever I have occasion to drive across the Malvern Hills I take a delight in reading them on the sign-posts; Leintwardine and Hoarwithy, Clehonger and Brampton Bryan, Bishop's Frome and Ewyas Harold, Much Marcle and Mansell

Gamage, Stretton Grandison standing close by Stretton Sugwas. And here's one to make you smile: Weston Beggard. And here's another which Dickens never knew, or he would assuredly have named a character after it: Edvin Loach!

THE HAPPIEST HUNTING-GROUND for place-names is perhaps *Horse and Hound*, or any of the small country newspapers which still publish reports of the doings of the local pack. Turn over the pages now at this season when dog-foxes go a-courting and, being roused far from home by the Hunt next morning, cross half-a-dozen parishes before they are lost or caught. " Our pilot," you read —which in excruciating huntingese means the fox—" turned left-handed just short of Laloo Farm." Why Laloo, a mournful-melodious name for a lonely farmhouse? Although it's within a few miles of my own house I cannot tell you. The six-inch-to-the-mile ordnance map is full of such oddities, in which local history, personal history, and folk-lore are inextricably mixed; but in the hunting reports you get half a dozen of them crowded into a single paragraph, and the English countryside spreads out invitingly before you: " Reynard turned sharp under the lee of Trafalgar Wood "—which tells you when the wood was first planted—" ran through Dogleg Spinney, across the Hoo and into Lyppiatts, where finding the earth stopped he circled Towbury and crossed Bromsberrow Common skirting Woodmancote at Waterloo Corner."

There are hundreds of ' Waterloos ' scattered over the country-side, just as there are innumerable ' Trafalgars '. The ' Jubilee Woods ', which you find fairly often too, were mostly planted by landowners to celebrate Queen Victoria's long reign. Thus you can read English history in the pages of *Horse and Hound*. During the war I met an exile in West Africa who although he had never been a hunting man (and oddly enough was opposed to blood-sports) had it sent out to him every week so that he could read the reports of hunting runs. They sang to him of the woods and lanes and meadows of his homeland; I have a fancy that sometimes he wept over them at night. . . . " Our pilot, a straight-necked un, swam the brook which runs through Bull Pates Meadow, headed for Lower Slaughter, crossed Lovers' Lane, and with the bitch pack screaming hard upon his Holy Water Sprinkler raced to the summit of Cockpit Hill where hounds caught him not twenty yards from Dawn o' Day. . . ."[1]

'HOLY WATER SPRINKLER' was borrowed, I suspect, from some very old book on hunting. You find it in Manwood's *Treatise and Discourse of the Lawes of the Forest*, printed in 1598. There is a whole long chapter devoted to " the Apt and Meete Terms of Hunting," which instructs the Forester in the different expressions which he must use for all the parts of the different creatures. " Of a Hart you shall say the tayle, of a Buck the single, of a Boar the wreath, of a Wolf his stern, of the Hare the scut, of a Fox his brush or Holy Water Sprinkler."

It was important, apparently, not to make a mistake in these matters. A Hart's track was called the slot, a Buck's the dewe, a Boar's the tract or treading, a Fox's the footing, and " Of a Hare, diversely, for when she is in plain fields, she soteth; when she chaceth about to deceave the hounds, then she dubleth; when she beateth a hard high way, where you may yet find and perceave her footing, there she pricketh: Also in time of snow, we say the trace of a Hare."

Then there were the Nouns of Assembly:

" Forresters and good Woodmen use to say, A herd of Harts, a Bevie of Roes, a Sounder of Swine, a rout of Wolves, a richesse of Martens, a brace of Bucks, a couple of Rabets or Conies . . ."

When the beasts of the chase were in their lairs, you spoke of them thus: " A Hart harboureth, a Buck lodgeth, a Roe beddeth, a Hare is seated or formed, a Conie sitteth, a Fox kenneleth." When your hounds drove them forth you had " dislodged the Buck, started the Hare, roused the Hart, unkennelled the Fox, bolted the Conie."

---

[1] This is presumably a hilltop; and what a delightful name for it!

And so it goes on. Even the mating of animals had to be spoken of in the precise terms ordained by tradition. " A Hart goeth to rut, a Roe goeth to his tourne, a Boar goeth to the brimme, a Hare and Conie to the buck, a Fox to clicketting." And there was an even stranger formality of Foresters' speech:

" This is a thing heighly to be observed, that the ordure of every beast of chase and venerie hath his proper tearm: the reason is because that their ordure and excrements are one principal mark, whereby the good Forresters and Woodmen do know the place of their feed. And also their estate: so that a Forrester or Woodman in talk, or in making of their reports, whal be often constrained to rehearse the same; and therefore you that onderstand, that of an Hart, and of all Deare, the ordure is called fewmets, or few mishing; of a Hare, crottals or cratising; of a Boar, the lesses; of a Fox, and all other vermin, the syants."

As for the antlers of deer, there seems to have been no end to the weird and outlandish words used to describe them: " The lowest Antlier is called the Brow Antlier, and the next above that Surroial; in a Buck they say, Bur Beame, Braunch, Advauncers, Palme and Shellers."

The Court Huntsman obviously had to be a pretty learned fellow, and was doubtless a stickler for etiquette, as old butlers are, who would sternly reprove a young keeper or kennelman for speaking of a Buck in his third year as a Sore (whereas he should have said Sorrell) or of a Doe in her second year as a Fawn (whereas the right phrase was "a Pricket's sister.") A second-year Roe ceased to be a kid and became a Gyrle; and in its third year it became a Hermuse.

What a sonority of strange words must have been heard about the kitchens of a great lord, when the huntsmen and grooms told their tale of the day's doings and the cook hastened to prepare the supper and the servants ran to and fro in response to his behests, which were framed in terms just as curious as the hunting-terms I have quoted from Manwood. For instance, a quaint book called

The Accomplisht Lady's Delight catalogues " the proper terms of carving a fish." Here they are: You

" *barb* a lobster, *chine* a salmon, *culpon* a trout, *sauce* a tench, *fin* or *frush* a chevin, *tranch* a sturgeon, *side* a haddock, *splay* a bream, *splat* a pike, *string* a lamprey, *tame* a crab, *transon* an eel, *tusk* a barbel."

How splendid it must have sounded, before an enormous feast, when the chef shouted to his minions, " Barb me a lobster, you; and you, make haste, tusk me a barbel and tame me a couple of crabs ! "

I have never eaten a barbel, tusked or otherwise, and I don't think I should like to; for another ancient work, *The Treatyse of Fysshinge wyth an Angle*, warns that " it is a queasy meete and a peryllous for mannys body. For comynly he giveth an introduxion to Ye Fevers. And Yf he be eaten rawe, he may be cause of mannys death." A later writer, George Smith, whose book is called *The Gentleman Angler*, declares of barbel " Their spawn is surfeiting and dangerous, and whosoever eats thereof will break out in Blotches and red Spots, and loathe his Meat, lose his Appetite, and be extremely disorder'd."

But fresh meat of any kind was rare in the days when Manwood wrote his Treatise about the stern Laws of the Forest and when the *Accomplisht Lady* instructed her cooks how to speak with proper respect of the fish they prepared for her table; so doubtless barbel were tusked and thrown into the hotchpotch to the accompaniment of these curious words which sound like incantations and which represent the very hotchpotch of our language: fragments of Norman French, scraps of Italian, flavourings of Old German, gobbets of Old English, Anglo-Saxon, Celtic, Latin: words of the chase, words of the kitchen, herbalists' words, wisewomen's words, words used by foresters and farmers, by gardeners and falconers, monkish words, words invented by untaught peasants as they went to their labour in the morning and heard the birds singing to whom as yet the ' scholards ' had given no names.

Some of these ancient words of limited or specialised use have vanished altogether, blown away like thistledown on the winds of time; some have stuck on to our language like the burrs on the Colonel's stockings, odd excrescences; others have altered or modified their meanings and although their origins are forgotten have become the stuff of our common speech or uncommon poetry. They are our passion-wingèd ministers of thought, they belong to the ghostly company which Edward Thomas when he first began to write verses summoned about him in his invocation to the English words:

> *Light as dreams,*
> *Tough as oak,*
> *Precious as gold,*
> *As poppies and corn*
> *Or an old cloak.*
> *Strange and sweet*
> *Equally*
> *And familiar to the eye*
> *As the dearest faces*
> *That a man knows*
> *Or as lost homes are.*

But there are yet others no longer familiar but not quite lost, nor buried too deep for us to find them in the archives of manuscript or old print, of which when we hear old men talking we can catch a faint echo now and then. Our old men had them from their grandfathers, who in turn perhaps had them in the days of their youth from some good-for-nothing wandering fellow who had known when *he* was a boy some famous grand-dad who loved to tell tales. . . . And so the long chain stretches back to the man who first invented this word or that one, the poet for-ever unknown who saw one day the little gay flower we call the campion, and named it Bridget-in-her-bravery because—who knows?—his wife that day was dressed up to go to the Fair! Back, back to some delver long ago who saw the earth stirring and crumbling in his tilled patch so hard-won from the waste, and pouncing upon the burrow caught

sight of the velvety black muzzle and the splayed-out paws. An
oont, he named it; and leaning on his spade, seeing the little beast's
handiwork, half-complaining, half-amused, uttered for the first
time that rough old word which is half-way between a grunt and
a grumble: Oontitoomps, he said.

SURELY we have a native genius for words, and especially for those
we give to the commonest things. Consider ' daisy ', the Day's
Eye; what exquisite precision! We could sit down with all the
dictionaries for a score of years and never find another pair of
words which, being strung together, so accurately and beautifully
described the flower. Then candytuft, cowslip, periwinkle, holly-
hock, honeysuckle, loosestrife, snowdrop, redhot-poker, ladysmock,
love-in-the-mist were all invented by poets; and snapdragon perhaps by a poet who was also a child. It is much better than the
Greek *Antirrhinum*, just as ' wavewind ' is better than the Latin
Convolvulus. And ' gillyflower ', which comes from Old French
(*gilofre*, a clove, because of its scent) is immensely improved in
English. So is ' dandelion ', which the scholars tell us is a corruption
of *Dent-de-lion*—the plant was so called in French on account of its
toothed leaves. If this is really so, by what a happy English accident
did we hit upon ' dandelion ', a word which has all the flaunting
splendour of that golden-maned dandy! But I do not think the
French often speak of it as *Dent-de-lion* nowadays. They call it
Pissenlit, because of its supposed diuretic properties if you drink an
infusion of it as tea, or a wine made from its flower-heads, before
you go to bed! (Old Gerard, however, who ought to have known
about such things, makes no mention of these properties in his
Herbal. He doesn't have any medical use for the dandelion, but
he describes it charmingly: Upon every stalke standeth a floure
greater than that of Succorie, but double, & thicke set together, of
colour yellow, which is turned into a round downy blowbal that is
carried away by the wind.)

Almost always, when we have taken the foreign name of a
flower and matched it to our own tongue, we have managed to

improve upon it. The Cornish people, for instance, being quite unable to pronounce the botanical name of their common cliff-side plant, *Mesembryanthemum*, call it Sally-my-handsome, which is very much nicer. Then there is *Galinsoga parviflora*, an introduction from Peru which recently became naturalised in London, spread all over the place, and is now a pernicious weed, as common as groundsel, in many suburban gardens and allotments. Gardeners, schoolchildren and others became interested in it and took the trouble to find out its Latin name—for being a new arrival it had no English one. *Galinsoga* didn't mean much to them, so they christened it 'Gallant Soldier' and 'Gallant Soldier' it will surely remain. (As children we called plantains 'soldiers', perhaps because they stood up so straight and their round heads were reminiscent of busbies.) But 'Gallant Soldier' is a splendid name; and no doubt before long some learned lexicographer will incorporate it in his dictionary, and it will be as respectable an English word as dandelion.

Or as primrose,—which our schoolmasters tell us comes from *Prima Rosa*, the first rose. But there is something mysterious here, for primroses are truly *prim*. They are the primmest of all wild flowers, they have a maidenly and virginal air which Shakespeare perceived when he wrote of them in *The Winter's Tale*:

> *Pale primroses,*
> *That die unmarried ere they can behold*
> *Bright Phœbus in his strength—a malady*
> *Most incident to maids;*

Was it really an accident that the corruption of the Latin words produced so marvellously apt a name? Or was it a stroke of genius on the part of some poet for ever anonymous? Certainly apt names are sometimes invented by accident. A few years ago a little polar bear was born in the London Zoo. Not knowing what to call her, her keepers joined together their own Christian names, Bruce and Sam, with Sam spelt backwards: Brumas. What a name! You can hear the sea's surge and the wind's sigh in it—Brumas!—and almost feel the wet cold brume of her native land. We must not, however, conclude from this that zoo keepers are always poets. Brumas's splendid and savage mother was called Ivy; and she was spoken of by the keepers as Our Ive.

V

IT WAS the first daisy of the year that set me thinking about the aptness of flower-names. It also started me hunting the hedge-rows to see how many humble and intrepid flowers I could find in bloom on a frosty, snow-sprinkly afternoon in February. My tally was nine. The daisy came from my lawn, which in summer shame-lessly proliferates daisies; groundsel from my flower-beds, where likewise it is a summer resident; and I found a single clear-blue periwinkle in flower on the garden wall. There were a few sweet violets on a sheltered hedgebank, and both the dead nettles, red and white, which are the most persistent in flowering of all our plants, I should imagine: there's not a month in the year when you cannot find them fully out. Thus they tie with the gorse, said to blossom whenever kissing is in fashion and therefore at all seasons, snow or shine. A sprig of gorse, whose two or three stunted and reluctant flowers suggested it was not an ideal day for courtship, made my Number Seven, and Number Eight was a single, precocious colts-foot which belongs to March and shouldn't really have been in flower at all. I have never loved the coltsfoot because in my childhood an infusion of it was frequently served up to me under the name of Coltsfoot Tea. It was supposed to cure coughs, hence its scientific name *Tussilago*. I must quote Gerard again:

"A decoction made of the greene leaves and roots, or else a syrap thereof, is good for the cough. The fume of the dried leaves taken through a funnell or tunnell, burned upon coles, effectually helpeth those that are troubled with the shortnesse of breath and fetch their winde thicke and often. Being taken in manner as they take tobaco, it mightily prevaileth against the diseases aforesaid."

And well it may; for they smoke coltsfoot cigarettes in some country districts still and it was one of the herbs with which inveterate smokers during war-time shortage would dilute their pipe-tobacco, vying with each other it seemed to produce so stinking a mixture that railway carriages would empty because of it and the inhabitants of air-raid shelters go out and face death from the skies rather than be suffocated by it.

My ninth and last flower was like a tiny tassel of red wool upon a bare hazel-bough; but a real flower nevertheless, the female part of the hazel, whose catkins, lambikins or lambs' tails as countryfolk call them represent the males and provide pollen when the April sun opens them and the April bees get busy. When "apples be ripe and nuts be brown" my little scarlet tassel will be a plump nut, wearing as it hangs on the hazel-bough the pretty green elf-cap of its kind.

SIGNS OF SPRING are welcome at this season, even such unobtrusive ones as the Spring Usher moths upon the tree trunks and palings. They are difficult to see unless you are practised at it: indeed I am sure that practice, and not sharpness of sight, is the chief factor in this business of noticing things. I knew an old naturalist who was so shortsighted that he couldn't read a car's number-plate at a dozen yards; but he would recognise more humble flowers and inconspicuous insects in the course of a country walk than anybody else I have ever been out with. The Colonel even when age and whisky had bleared his sight could spot a hare lying still in the furrow of a ploughed field. Moths on a fence are just as good a match for their surroundings; they sometimes look like knots in the wood. Once in pursuit of my bughunting hobby I was searching some split-chestnut palings in a suburban road when a policeman cocked an eye at me and demanded what I was doing. It was during the war, when even the most harmless actions, if they were in the least unusual, took on a sinister significance. I asked the policeman why he wanted to know. He replied: "If you don't want to tell me I can always charge you with being a suspected person." But when I explained I was looking for moths he didn't believe me, and I had to make him do what Chesterton's Father Brown would have done in similar circumstances. Father Brown, of course, was a natural detective because he possessed the simple logic of innocence. If he saw anybody behaving unaccountably he would behave in exactly the same way himself, and so discover what the person was up to.

I therefore persuaded the poor policeman to act as I had been doing; I made him walk along the fence and look for moths. But he couldn't see them! I had to take his hand and guide his finger to what he thought was merely a roughness in the wood so that at last he touched it and it flew away. But he was not shortsighted. He was simply unpractised at looking for moths, though doubtless he was very good at seeing suspected persons.

A BOY with a jamjar is a surer sign of spring than my little Spring Ushers. It contains frog-spawn, and the egg-laying of frogs is dependent upon the climatic conditions during several weeks. Only if we've had a mild, wet February (which I think generally results in an early spring) do the frogs begin to lay in mid-March.

We all, I suppose, were fascinated by frog-spawn when we were young, pulled off lumps of the jellied mass, dumped them in jamjars, and bore them home; watched the tiny black spot, which was Life, appear, grow, take shape among the cloudy jelly like an Idea forming in the mind. . . . Then the jelly disintegrates, the black pinhead sprouts a tail and wriggles it, hind legs emerge, and at this stage the tadpole, if you hold it up vertically with the underside towards you, bears a remarkable resemblance to a Humpty-Dumpty—though, of course, it is a Humpty-Dumpty with a tail. It doesn't look in the least like a frog, anyhow; but when at last the change happens it is swift and complete. Gills for underwater breathing are replaced by lungs; the skin is cast, the external mouth disappears as if it were a mask torn away from a mummer, the fat tummy flattens, forelegs come forth, tail vanishes. The thing is a little frog suddenly: a paddock, as we used to say, for we knew Herrick's " Child's Grace ":

> *Here a little child I stand*
> *Heaving up my either hand,*
> *   Cold as paddocks though they be*
> *Here I lift them up to Thee,*
> *For a benison to fall*
> *On our meat and on us all. Amen!*

In the North Country, and in Scotland, frogs and toads are all

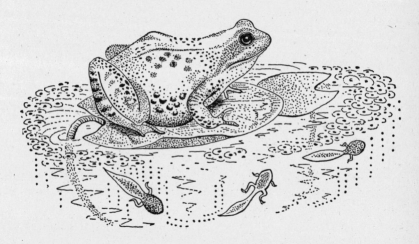

called paddocks impartially; but we must have got the word from Herrick, for I do not think it is used in the Midlands. I like 'paddock' better than 'frog', I think, and I certainly prefer 'eft' to 'newt'. 'Eft' is a pretty, quaint word, matching the quaint creature which used sometimes to share our jamjars with the tadpoles. Newts, of course, have their own tadpoles, and develop in much the same way as frogs; we weren't aware of this until what we had thought was an ordinary tadpole began to take on the lineaments of some minor dragon, and one day astonished us by becoming a fully-fledged Warty Newt, which is a much stranger animal than anything in heraldry. Enlarge him a hundred times, and even Saint George would turn and run. He is also known as the Great Water Newt, and the French pleasantly call him the Crested Triton. He is purplish brown on top with black spots; he has a bright orange belly and fingers and toes prettily marked with black and yellow; a white throat; and (in the breeding season) a fine crest running down his back from the top of his head to the tip of his tail. His lady has no such crest but makes up for it by having her underparts picked out in vivid yellow and black, like a leopardskin.

I haven't seen a newt for years, because I haven't looked for one; but my recollection is that there were certain Newty Ponds in which one had only to dip one's net a few times to be sure of catching one. Other ponds were barren of newts; but this may have been because we fished them at the wrong time of year, for newts are aquatic mainly during the breeding season; thereafter you generally find them near the pond in cracks of the ground, among grass, or under stones.

But when you are grown up you no longer find them. They, and the little black tadpoles, belong to childhood and its wonderment. They are not for us, any more. They are for the boy with the jamjar, who hates tapioca milk-puddings and describes them as frog-spawn; MUMMY I SHALL BE SICK. But the genuine frog-spawn has no such effect upon him. He holds flaccid slimy chunks of it in grubby wet hands ('cold as paddocks though they be'!); he crams it into the jamjar; he puts the jamjar on a shelf and there it stays, to the dismay of parents, while the poor tadpoles languish in the dirty water, martyrs to the awakening curiosity of the human male, sacrifices to science.

VI

Pʜᴜᴛᴛᴛ! The first sound is so slight—it is the faintest imaginable flip—that only by reason of my mis-spent youth I immediately realise its import. The second sound, right over my head, is a very distinct *whoo-oo-sh* followed by a brief rustle in the boughs of the apple-tree which leans over my garden wall. Some torn-off leaves come tumbling down; but fortunately there are no feathers. A faintly-puzzled cock blackbird breaks off his singing and leisurely flies away.

He is luckier than he knows; for when, sallying out, I pounce upon the tow-headed eleven-year-old I discover that the weapon was fairly lethal: there are seven, no, nine notches on the handle. The prong is cut from a stout hazel—*we* used to shape ours out of the tops of cigar-boxes, of which I can still recollect the aromatic smell; but, of course, cigar-boxes are rarer today.

The elastic is of the square-sided black sort, somewhat like liquorice and apt to be confused with liquorice if it has inhabited a sticky pocket for a few weeks. There were other kinds of elastic which were offered to us by shopkeepers lacking in understanding. We scorned them, holding them to be fit only for girls' garters, and always insisted that the only true catty-lacky was the square-sided, costing, in those days, three-ha'pence a yard.

The ends of this excellent elastic (I now notice with an appraising eye) are neatly compressed through grooves nicked into the top of each prong, the prongs then being whipped with waxed string. The sling itself is made of chamois-leather, which is very superior and professional: *we* used to cut the tongues out of old and not-so-old shoes. The notches on the handle are of different sizes, and this, I fear, may have some dark significance. I resolve not to inquire into it.

Instead I discourse upon the sacrosanct nature of blackbirds in the breeding season. The tow-headed urchin stares at me with a resentful and defensive stare which uncomfortably reminds me of my own expression some 35 years ago. Do I confiscate the catapult, thus saving, perhaps, the lives of a few beloved songsters? I recollect my hatred, almost murderous, of one such confiscator, and I realise that I am not really cut out for the role.

I therefore hand back the weapon, and recommend target-practice on tins. I know quite well, however, that no normal boy —and this one is aggressively normal—will get any satisfaction out of target-practice on tins. The normal boy requires a living target: he requires, to put it brutally, to see the feathers fly. Such a spectacle nowadays causes me deep distress; but then I am no longer eleven.

Catapults are better than coshes, I reassure myself; though on reflection I am not sure that they are less murderous. The word is Greek for "to hurl against" and a well-made catty can hurl a round pebble from the brook against Goliath or any other sizeable target with extraordinary force.

Gypsies use catapults in their gang-warfare, and I know one Cyclopian fellow called Black Alfred who lost his left eye by reason of his opponent's good marksmanship. Moreover it is not necessary to use a stone; a bullet is better and in my youth I possessed a device like a pair of forceps with hollow and rounded ends which fitted tightly together and had a small hole in the top into which one could pour molten lead.

The molten lead was usually an ex-Highlander, Uhlan, Dragoon or Horse Guard broken off his stand in the course of some skirmish of the toy soldiers. He was melted down upon the fire and poured into the curious instrument—can it have been made for the purpose? —out of which, when the lead had cooled, came a heavy, round bullet. This was deadlier than any pebble.

I made a score of such bullets in readiness for the arrival of the so-called Garden Gun which I'd seen advertised in some boys' paper about the time of my tenth birthday. NO LICENCE REQUIRED, said the advertisement. SHOOTS ACCURATELY WITH STONES OR LEAD PELLETS.

Alas, when the Garden Gun arrived it consisted simply of an ash walking stick, not quite straight, into one end of which was screwed a metal prong; at the other end was a kind of trigger and a clip into which the sling of a catapult could be fitted. The elastic, of course, was tied to the ends of the metal prong. I had little faith in the weapon, and less faith after I had fired it, because it was the only gun I have ever owned which could shoot round corners.

The first experimental discharge, aimed at a post at the bottom of the garden, produced a neat, round hole in a shirt which hung upon a neighbour's clothes-line, in the garden which ran parallel with ours. The second produced a tinkling of glass which I did not wait to investigate. SHOOTS ACCURATELY WITH LEAD PELLETS. . . .

I ran into the house, and hid, and nursed my first bitter disillusion about the integrity of advertisers. The Garden Gun found its way into the junk room among the jigsaw puzzles which had the most important pieces missing, and the clockwork toys that had broken their mainsprings, and the Teddy Bear that used to grunt when one pressed his tummy, but had lost his grunt when I was about seven.

VII

THE WEIR is almost the only one of my boyhood haunts that doesn't change with the years. The woods I birdnested in are mostly cut down, the little new houses have sprawled out over the fields, much of the river-bank has been stripped of its willows by the destructive bulldozers of the River Board. But Elmbury Weir on the River Severn still looks the same, smells the same, makes the same dull thunder which if you listen to it long enough becomes a kind of noisy silence.

In March the elvers like short lengths of bootlace wriggle up the slack water at the edge of the current, and the elver-fishers go out by moonlight with their scoop-like nets of cheese-cloth to gather a profitable harvest of these tiny eels. There are salmon too, silver as new-minted coins, though for some reason they are uncatchable on rod and line. They swim on up the Severn and give sport to the anglers in the upper reaches; but at Elmbury they are only taken once in a blue moon more or less by accident by men fishing for pike or by small boys who are the darlings of the gods.

This is all the more strange since the Wye, which shares the Severn's estuary, and runs almost parallel with it on the other side of the Malvern Hills, is one of the best salmon-rivers in the world. In 1923 a young girl, Miss Doreen Davy, caught there a monster of 59½ lbs.; that's nearly the record salmon for England: a 60-pounder just beats it. But the record for Scotland is no less than 67 lbs., and this is how it stands in the fishing books that concern themselves with such things:

" *Salmon.*   67 lbs., caught in the River Nith, 1812, by Jock Wallace, a poacher."

So Mr. Wallace's fame has lasted for nearly 150 years, but because of his achievement, or his monumental piece of luck, his addiction to poaching is likewise remembered till Kingdom come. I wonder how the record became known. A poacher wouldn't normally advertise the fact that he had caught a whopper; but this salmon, I suppose, was *such* a whopper that he simply couldn't resist taking it down to the pub, and weighing it on the pub-scales, and celebrating it with a dram or two, and taking the consequences, whatever they might be.

I've never understood Iago's riddling lines spoken to Desdemona:

> *She that in wisdom never was so frail*
> *To change the cod's head for the salmon's tail*;

unless cod, being sea-fish and therefore for most of the inhabitants of England scarce and expensive, was regarded as the greater delicacy. Shakespeare certainly knew about the salmon of the Wye; for Fluellen says " There is a river in Macedon; and there is moreover a river at Monmouth . . . and there is salmons in both."

These famous salmon were also the subject of a remarkable legal action which the Law books call Chesterfield versus Harris and which, in the year 1906, fluttered the wigs of the learned judges in the Chancery Division, and of the Lord Justices of Appeal, and even the very important wig of the Lord Chancellor of England. It happened that for longer than anybody could remember the freeholders of a little Wye-side village called Hoarwithy had been accustomed to take salmon out of an 8-mile stretch of the Wye. They believed that the King had granted them this right; but they couldn't remember which King, nor when. It was certainly true they'd fished free for generations, and nobody had interfered with them. There were certain curious conditions attaching to the fishing: " If they shall have taken any salmons they ought themselves to bring the same salmons to the Fish Board at Hoarwithy and remain there by the space of two hours before they bring the same salmons to any market or fair." The Fish Board was a slab outside the village inn; and any pregnant woman in the village had the right to cut a piece out of any salmon displayed there without payment! However, the old custom fell into disuse, and the fishermen got into the habit of taking their catches direct to the fishmongers at Hereford. This gave the Wye landlords their chance; the Earl of Chesterfield and others brought an action to restrain the Free Fishers. The case lasted seven days in the Chancery Court and the judge found in favour of the fishermen; but the Court of Appeal reversed the judgement, and so the persistent villagers of Hoarwithy carried their case to the House of Lords. Men who had never left their native village travelled adventurously to London-town and boldly stood up for their rights before the wigged Counsel and the grave judges. Their good broad Hereford accents must have brought a breath of fresh air into the stuffy Lords! At home, everybody in the village followed the case as eagerly as people follow the fortunes of their local fooball team. How sad it is to record that Hoarwithy lost!

"Your Lordships," said Counsel for the landlords, "are asked to assume a grant which did not exist, to a corporation which never existed, in order to assume a right which is unknown in English law. . . ."

All of which was doubtless true. There is something splendid all the same about this David-and-Goliath affair, and I don't much like to think of the homecoming of the village stalwarts, crestfallen that night in the village pub, telling a bewildered tale of how the men who "fight by shuffling papers" had beaten them in a battle of which they didn't even know the rules!

ALTHOUGH the salmon are so disobliging at Elmbury, its weir is a kind of lucky dip from which, when schoolboys chuck out their random lines, they are liable to conjure all kinds of unexpected fishes. In May the twaite migrate up the river from the sea. They are very pretty fish, silvery-green, and weighing up to a couple of pounds. They will take a fly, but the boys catch them on a white feather or a hank of red wool attached to a bare hook. There are also flounders to be caught on worms. They are not often big enough to eat (though as a child I once took a monster which I sold to the fishmonger for sixpence, a sum for which in those days I could buy six hooks with gut attached!) Mostly they are of the size that can be accommodated in jamjars; and there our captives unhappily spent the brief remainder of their lives, lying on their sides at the bottom of the jar and looking up at us with a pair of reproachful eyes set, most oddly, both at the same side of the head.

Doubtless we perceived, young as we were, that this provision of two eyes on one side was not simply a whim of the Almighty but was the only sensible arrangement for a creature which spends nine-tenths of its time lying sideways upon the mud. In fact, however, the flounder isn't born like this. When it hatches from its egg it is the same shape as any ordinary fish—say a baby cod. As it grows up its cranium gradually rotates, carrying the orbit of the eye with it, until at last the left eye joins the other one on the right hand side of the head. This must be an odd experience; but it is an inescapable one if you are born a flounder and when it is completed you are well equipped to see what is going on as you lie upon the river-bottom, mud-coloured dark-side-up to camouflage you from your foes.

The flavour of the flounder has been likened to that of boiled wadding; and its chief claim to fame is that its female lays very nearly a million eggs (970,000, according to some expert who invented a way of counting them). This is more than any other flat-fish lays; and no doubt accounts for the fact that Elmbury Weir provides an unlimited number of flounders for small boys to catch. Grown-up anglers naturally despise them; and water-bailiffs heartily wish that there were no such fishes for since they belong properly to the sea they are not coarse-fish within the meaning of the Act and so may be taken in the close season. This gives the small boys (and a few unprincipled elders) a good excuse when the water-bailiff comes along and reproves them for fishing at the wrong time of year. " Only catching flounders, Mister!—flounders and ee-uls! " But if I know small boys, they are fishing for whatever they can catch.

THE STRANGEST of all the inhabitants of the Weir is surely the lamprey, a mottled, hideous-looking creature about three feet long, with a sucking disc in its mouth, with which it attaches itself to other fishes, to stones, even to passing boats or to the sill of the Weir itself. You cannot catch it, of course, by ordinary fishing, but you can sometimes hook it out with a gaff, and a good cook will make a very tasty dish of it, though I believe this depends on a special recipe which only a few old Elmbury families still possess.

It was upon *lamperns*, I imagine, and not lampreys, that Henry the First surfeited himself till he died. These are much smaller, but are regarded as a greater delicacy. Incidentally, the city of Gloucester has an ancient obligation to send " a dish of lamperns to the King on his succession and annually at Christmas." King John fined the aldermen of the city 40 marks because " they did not pay him sufficient respect in the matter of his lamperns." The more dutiful Corporation during Queen Victoria's reign sent her a pie weighing 20 lbs " filled with Severn lampreys, decorated with truffles in aspic jelly and crayfish upon gold spears."

The sturgeon is another Royal perquisite which has been caught in the past in Elmbury Weir, though not for many years now. I was once told by some excited children that there were " four or five enormous sturgings playing merry blazes in our bathing-place," and I hurried across there only to find a school of porpoises which had swum up from the sea.

It was delightful to watch them playing; and when I swam out to them they accepted me as another porpoise and played with me, barging me in a friendly way and splashing within a few feet of my face. I believe they are perfectly harmless, though they might knock the wind out of you if they became very boisterous.

After a few days in the Weir they vanished as suddenly as they had come; but ever since then I have felt that it is a place where almost any water-monster might appear, a Scotch kelpie or a Welsh afanc or Leviathan himself; even a Mermaid from the South Seas. But if *she* comes, sure enough some oaf will say to himself, as usual: " Here's something strange; let's kill it "—and run home to fetch his gun.

As BEAUTIFUL as any mermaid are the otters which play in the swift weir water on summer evenings when they are teaching their cubs the ring-a-ring-a-roses tail-chasing games which otters love. I can never understand how anybody over 25 can find otter-hunting more enjoyable than otter-watching. It is a cruel and unlovely exercise, though I don't want to have it stopped by Act of Parliament. I am implacably opposed to all the Antis who want to invoke the Law to stop other people doing things which they themselves don't approve of. But if the otter-hunters go on as they have been doing recently I think they'll probably get a ducking sooner or later at the hands of some infuriated spectators; and it might do them good. They hunt bitch-otters heavily in cub, and kill small cubs (though probably this is unavoidable) and instead of leaving the hounds to do the job, as foxhunters properly do, they seek to form what they call a ' stickle ' in the otter's path—four or five men with poles standing across a shallow part of the stream—so that the poor little beast, in a small river anyhow, is not so much hunted as murdered. Not long ago, having hunted a bitch-otter for an hour and a half near my home, they lost her in a deep holt under the bank from which she could not be bolted. They proceeded to draw off the water at the mill below, until her holt was exposed and she was killed, not in the water but in the thick mud of the river-bed, through which she could only flounder with the hounds splashing at her rudder. This exhibition deeply offended a number of farm-labourers who witnessed it; and I found it difficult to believe that anybody could be so insensitive as to find any satisfaction in it. However the otter-hunters were delighted with

their sport; and they all cut another notch on their poles to remember it by.

I ALWAYS regard with suspicion accounts of wild animals attacking
men. If they are wounded or cornered of course they will do so;
but experienced big-game hunters have told me that even the
great carnivores are generally only too anxious to run away. In
Britain almost all our native animals are timid, and I have found it
very difficult to believe the occasional tales I have read of foxes,
weasels, badgers and wild cats showing fight. Recently, however,
I had the job of going through the papers of a very accurate and
careful naturalist [1] who died not long ago. Among them I found
a genuine record of *otters* attacking humans without apparent reason.
It is so remarkable that I quote it *verbatim*, in the terse impersonal
phrases of the original notes:

" C. Whitfield killed 2 otters in withy pit at Hempstead near
Gloucester with sickle. He was walking directly behind boy
named Brint. Male otter made to attack Brint. Whitfield killed
it with blow from sickle. At once female made to attack Brint,
reared on hind legs and hissed. Whitfield killed her with several
blows. Male 11 lbs., fine coat, female 12 lbs., teats all dry, hair
very short round mammæ, poor condition, hair on back good,
uterus empty. Otters could have escaped in any direction (22/2/32)."

Almost certainly the otters had cubs nearby, though the cubs
had apparently been weaned. Nevertheless it seems extraordinary
that they should have attacked the osier-cutter and his boy instead
of slinking into hiding among the withies. I believe this record to
be unique, and I set it down here partly for that reason and partly
because the quotation is an example to all naturalists in accurate
note-taking. Not a word is wasted; not a relevant fact is omitted.

But I do not like to think of those brave little beasts being
hacked to death with a sickle; and I wonder what would have
happened if the man and boy had stood their ground and *waited*.
Possibly the otters were doing no more than making a demonstra-

[1] Dr. Oliver H. Wild.

tion in force. In any case their courage was that of dwarfs defying giants. How do we *look* to the smaller beasts of the field? Horrifying, hideous, and huge, I should think: like space-men might appear to us. (Probably we exude a most offensive smell as well!) Above all, we must seem utterly *strange*. There is a description in W. H. Hudson's *Book of a Naturalist* of a midnight encounter between a badger and a policeman in west Cornwall, 'a giant six feet six in height, a mighty wrestler, withal a sober, religious man, himself a terror to all evil-doers in the place.' The policeman's beat extended on one side to the border of a wide, wild moor, 'and one very dark night last winter he was at this desolate spot when he heard the distant sound of a horse cantering over the ground. The heavy rains had flooded the land, and he heard the splash of the hoofs as the horse came towards him. "Who could this be out on horseback at twelve o'clock on a dark winter night?" he asked himself; and listened and waited while the sound grew louder and louder and came nearer and nearer, and he strained his eyes to see the figure of a man on horseback emerging from the gloom, and could see nothing. Then it suddenly came into his mind that it was no material horseman, but a spirit accustomed to ride at that hour in that place, and his hair stood up on his head like the bristles on a pig's back. "It almost lifted my helmet off," he confessed, and he would have fled, but his trembling legs refused to move. Then, all at once, when he was about to drop, fainting with extreme terror, the cause of the sound appeared—an old dog badger trotting over the flooded moor, vigorously pounding the water with his feet, and making as much noise as a trotting horse with his hoofs. The badger was seven or eight yards away when he first caught sight of him, and the badger, too, then saw a sublime and terrible creature standing motionless before him, and for a few moments they stared at one another; then the badger turned aside and vanished into the darkness.'

All encounters, all contacts, between men and animals seemed to Hudson to contain that element of terror and strangeness. They spoke no common language, they shared no common wisdom or experience, they were beings as incomprehensible to each other as Martians would be to men of this earth. One of the difficulties of a field-naturalist is to make the kind of approach to wild beasts which mitigates, or minimises, the appalling *shock* of seeing the human form at close quarters.

Still greater, of course, for most wild things, is the shock of being handled by the monster. Let me quote Hudson again, on the pipistrelle bat:

"Its wing is a bed and field of nerves so closely placed as to give the membrane the appearance of the finest, softest, shot silk. The brains of the creature, as it were, are carried spread out on its wings, and so exquisitely delicate is the sensitiveness of these parts that in comparison our finger-tips are no more quick of feeling than the thick tough hide of some lumbering pachyderm. The touch of a soft finger-tip on its wing is to a bat like the blow of a cheese or nutmeg grater on his naked body to a man."

Whenever I handle a bird or butterfly or bat or beast I try to remember that sentence. But however carefully I clasp my hand about the exhausted finch or the injured small animal I am fearfully conscious of the tremulous heart pulsing within my palm. It speaks to me of terror,—if only I could *tell* the small thing that this time at any rate it has nothing to be afraid of!

A FEW PEOPLE, but very few, have the patience, the gentleness, the capacity for quietude and the Franciscan quality of love in sufficient measure to tame a truly wild creature. Miss Len Howard, in her delightful study of *Birds As Individuals*, tells how she won the trust and in a sense perhaps the affection of the tits in her garden; doing so, she gradually came to recognise their distinctive characters and personalities, and her careful record seems to show that birds do not have standardised behaviour patterns common to a species and that they react to different circumstances or emergencies in different ways, as human beings do. I myself have seen wild red squirrels called out of their wood by a woman who lived in a cottage beside it, called *into her sitting-room*, climb on to her shoulder, and eat nuts from her hand. She too claimed to differentiate all the squirrels in the wood, to know their relationships and generations and to perceive personalities which lay beyond their instinctive reactions to sudden movement, proffered food, or unfamiliar surroundings.

But most of us, alas, when we say that a wild bird or animal is ' tame ' mean merely that it is apathetic. Extreme tiredness or acute hunger cause the apathy. Birds in a great frost become ' tame ' and dog-foxes weary after long mating-journeys become ' bold ' and are seen trotting across open fields in daylight. In this sense most wild creatures are tamest in the very early spring; for this is the season of greatest hunger, when the last of the berries and seeds are exhausted and the hibernating insects which were not well-hidden are all eaten up. On the high hills or the cold moorlands the last bite of grass has disappeared, and the new grass is not yet springing. The fat which was stored in the tissues of bird and beast against the long winter is used up too, so that you may have blue days in March, with ' spring in the air ', associated with extreme privation. On Dartmoor the ponies, cattle and sheep suffer their heaviest casualties at this season; for the green comes first upon the bogs, and hunger impels the animals towards what moormen call " the green eye ". The heather is black and withered, and the last of the herbage which survived in its shade has been nibbled away; spring shows itself first in the " green eye of the bog ", and the ponies are drawn on by it, a little farther, a little farther, a step too far. When they have taken that fatal last step they are often too weak, from long privation, to scramble out. In these harsher places, where the spring comes late, the spring is deadlier than the cruel winter itself.

Part Three

THE
CUCKOO'S STAY

I

" The cuckoo comes in April,
In May he sings all day.
In the middle of June he changes his tune,
In July he flies away."

So we never have more than three months of him: the best three
months of the year. He is a vulgar, ill-mannered parasite as I
suppose a good many true geniuses have been; but imagine what
April and May would be like without him, what an emptiness,
what a void! Suppose he became extinct: it would be as if a poet
had stopped singing; when people suddenly say to themselves
I shall never hear that voice again. I can forgive the cuckoo everything for the sake of his voice. The poor pipits that he battens upon
do not make their sacrifice in vain.

Gilbert White recorded that some cuckoos sing in C and some
in D: " two sang together, the one in D, the other in D sharp,
who made a disagreeable concert." My own ear is so bad that
I couldn't make the distinction. I cannot even whistle the very
simple air of the willow-warbler, which runs down the scale at
the end and has ' a dying fall ' like the strain which captivated Orsino.
I can talk to little owls, and persuade them to answer me, but that
is scarcely a musical accomplishment.

I wish I could even *describe* birds' songs; but it's a task too difficult
for most writers, though Gilbert White seemed to do it with such
ease; he wrote of the flycatcher's ' little inward wailing note ',

and of the sedge-warbler as 'a delicate polyglot'. The blackcap's
lovely song reminded him of some lines from *As You Like It* and
he described the wood-wren as making 'a sibilous shivering noise'
at the tops of the trees. The chiff-chaff filled him with amazement
that a bird no bigger than a man's thumb should fetch 'an echo
out of the Hanger with every note.' I think the chiff-chaff is the
only bird that ever bores me. His repetition is welcome in the
spring but becomes a burden in high summer, though his determination to make the world attend to his very tiny song is rather
endearing. He is so often invisible among the branches that I should
think it likely he got his name, through repeating it so indefatigably,
before the first bird-watchers learned to recognise his appearance.

QUITE a lot of birds have named themselves: the peewit and the
pipit for instance. Like the chiff-chaff, they were repeating their
two syllables when we were but Calibans lacking language, and
long before there were any men upon the earth the vociferous
cuckoo was shouting the word which was destined to become
associated with man's infidelities. He at any rate speaks a universal
tongue, his is the true Esperanto, he is *coucou* in French, *cuclillo* in
Spanish, *cuculo* in Italian, *cuculus* in Latin, *Kuck-uck* in German. I
don't know what the Moors and the Egyptians and the Sudanese
call him, but I expect it has much the same sound; for every year
he proclaims himself afresh, crying his name from South Africa to
Norway, from Finland to the Faroes, from the Caspian Sea to the
westernmost shores of the Atlantic. In China and Japan, in India
and in New Guinea, he has close cousins who doubtless cry
'cuckoo!' too; and since the subspecific name of one of them is
telephonus they presumably cry it just as loudly. He is a brash and
braggart bird, but however often he sings to us, he never becomes
a bore.

But we men named the nightingale! I don't know when, but at
least the name goes back to Chaucer, whose ardent young squire in
The Canterbury Tales:

The Cuckoo's Stay

So hote he loved that by nightertale
He slept namore than doth the nightingale.

The bird has sung in poetry ever since. It was Keats' 'light-wingèd Dryad of the trees', and in Shelley 'The lone nightingale Mourns not her mate with such melodious pain'. But for me the unforgettable nightingale is Swinburne's. In the Chorus in *Atalanta* he performs one of his best conjuring-tricks with words, he tosses up into the air three familiar ones, 'nightingale', 'brown' and 'bright', and, hey-presto, they come down like this:

> *And the* brown bright nightingale *amorous*
> *Is half-assuaged for Itylus,*
> *For the Thracian ships and the foreign faces,*
> *The tongueless vigil and all the pain.*

Incidentally, I much prefer the Old English word 'nightingale' to the pseudo-poetic, Grecian word Philomel, which polite versifiers in the eighteenth century considered to be a *sine qua non* in any bucolic ode. Philomel sounds very charming in an airy-fairy way until one is reminded (by Ivor Brown) of its similarity to Calomel, that old-fashioned family purge.

II

WHAT flower-name can we match with 'nightingale' for the ears' delight? Surely 'lily' is the loveliest of all. Again it is Ivor Brown, in one of his word-books, who draws attention to its unpleasing and rather extraordinary employment as an adjective ('lily-livered') and then gives for contrast an example of its beauty as used by Shakespeare in *Titus Andronicus*. The line follows close upon the most horrible stage-direction in the whole of playwriting: *Enter Lavinia, her hands cut off and her tongue cut out, and ravish'd*. But then Shakespeare, whose Hand of Glory is not very apparent in the play, comes in unmistakeably:

> O, *had the monster seen those lily hands*
> *Tremble like aspen leaves upon tha lute*

'GILDING the lily' has become one of those tendentious phrases used by tiresome people and implying disapproval of rouge and lipstick. One day on a brains trust we had a question couched in such terms; and my quick-witted friend Robert Henriques came back with "The lily doesn't have to cook, wash up, dust, scrub, deal with the nappies, stand in queues, get the children off to school. ... The lily can *afford* to be itself, ungilded. ..." But for once he was wrong. The lily can't. All flowers that depend upon insects for pollenisation take very good care to make themselves obvious and attractive, either by scent or by colour. Most of the true lilies (the white Arum *isn't* one, by the way) are in fact gilded by Nature herself; they go in for the bright shades between terra-cotta and red—much the same colours which girls use, and for much the same purpose! And if they are white, they have spots on the flowers leading to the pistil and stamens. But it is never very profitable for moralists to go to what the Victorians called the Natural Kingdom for their examples of how Mankind should behave. The brightly-coloured behinds of certain monkeys are probably the equivalent of a painted face in humankind. So is the peacock's tail and the ostrich's fine plumage. The spider's patience, which so impressed Robert Bruce, is devoted simply and solely to the purpose of trapping, binding and despatching its prey by the cruellest method known in the whole realm of nature. The hive-bees and those ants which the Bible recommends us sluggards to imitate provide in fact the most terrifying examples of totalitarianism in practice,— examples which Hitler, Mussolini and the Kremlin have striven to follow with varying degrees of success. As for the lilies of the field, which toil not neither do they spin yet Solomon in all his glory is not arrayed as one of them, they may be a very good example indeed but they are not an example which moralising mothers, who deplore ' gilding the lily ', would hold up to their daughters as a pattern of good behaviour to be strenuously followed!

If they want a symbol of respectability, they must choose the aspidistra; though, surprisingly, it turns out to be a lily too. Until I discovered this fact in an Encyclopædia of Gardening I could not for the life of me have told you what family it belonged to nor whence its misguided discoverer brought it to England. It is a native of Japan and its full name is *Aspidistra elatior*. Being a lily, and not as I supposed some dreary sort of fern, it must have a flower, and possibly a handsome one, for the *Liliaceae* do not as a rule hide their lights under a bushel. But I have never seen an aspidistra in bloom, and I doubt if I ever shall; for the poor thing generally languishes unwatered and unmanured in a green pot, without any drainage, which the Auctioneer, and nobody else, describes as a Jardinière; and in such circumstances I would not bloom for anyone, lily though I might be.

THE NAMES of herbs have a tang and a fragrance: marjoram, rose-

mary, pennyroyal, bergamot—which we grow in England mainly
for its decorative red flowers but which in France is used as a true
herb, for flavouring; they use it to make a sweet called *Bergamottes
de Nancy*, like acid-drops to look at, but with a taste delicious and
indescribable, that comes I suppose from the distilled essence of the
plant. English countryfolk seem to have forgotten the uses of
herbs; our Fathers of Old knew better, as Kipling reminds us
in those delightful verses through which he makes the herbs of
healing and of flavouring chant their own names to a homely
rhythm:

> *Excellent herbs had our fathers of old—*
> > *Excellent herbs to ease their pain—*
> *Alexanders and Marigold,*
> > *Eyebright, Orris and Elecampane.*
> *Basil, Rocket, Valerian, Rue,*
> > *(Almost singing themselves they run)*
> *Vervain, Dittany, Call-me-to-you—*
> > *Cowslip, Melilot, Rose of the Sun.*
> *Anything green that grew out of the mould*
> *Was an excellent herb to our fathers of old.*

' Call-me-to-you ' was the name by which the little wild pansy,
heartsease, was known to our fathers of old. I enjoy these many-
hyphened names of flowers, such as Jack-go-to-bed-at-noon for the
goatsbeard, and herb-o'-grace-o'-Sundays. But the most-hyphened
of all is ' Welcome-your-husband-whether-he-comes-home-drunk-
or-nay ', a piece of humane advice which also serves, in Somerset,
for the name of an acrid plant called the Biting Stonecrop.

OPHELIA handed out herb-o'-grace-o'-Sundays (which is a little
undistinguished thing that grows on the wall) with rosemary and
rue and the rank-smelling fennel. There was surely a herb-garden
at New Place, for the aromatic plants are always turning up in
Shakespeare,—

The Cuckoo's Stay

Hot lavender, mints, savory, marjoram;
The marigold, that goes to bed wi' th' sun,
And with him rises weeping;

The whole of that scene in *The Winter's Tale* is devoted to flowers; Perdita discusses the ' streak'd gillyvors ' (which were probably pinks, not wallflowers) and calls them ' Nature's bastards ', declaring:

I'll not put
The dibble in earth to set one slip of them,—

a phrase which any gardener might speak word for word today. Then comes the catalogue of the ' flowers of middle summer ', and then, as Perdita turns to the girls, that exquisite posy of the flowers o' the spring, the daffodils that come before the swallow dares, the violets dim, the pale primroses, the bold oxlips and all. . . . But I think Shakespeare's favourite flower was the cowslip. It's not the one he mentions most often (that's the violet, with the primrose a good second); but he always writes of cowslips with special tenderness and affection, with very close observation or very vivid memory. He must have *stared* at cowslips (' the freckled cowslip ' in *Henry V*, ' the cowslip's bell ' in *The Tempest*, ' drops i ' the bottom of a cowslip ' in *Cymbeline*—he surely saw them in some dewy dawn when he got up early or, like his Romeo, stayed out late). But the loveliest cowslips are in *A Midsummer-Night's Dream*:

The cowslips tall her pensioners be;
In their gold coats spots you see;
Those be rubies, fairy favours,
In those freckles live their savours.
I must go seek some dewdrops here,
And hang a pearl in every cowslip's ear.

The *Dream*, of course, is full of flowers:

131

Come Rain, Come Shine

I know a bank where the wild thyme blows,
Where oxlips and the nodding violet grows,
Quite over-canopied with luscious woodbine,
With sweet musk-roses, and with eglantine;
And there the snake throws her enamell'd skin,
Weed wide enough to wrap a fairy in;

So he'd seen that too: the sloughing of the grasssnake's lovely coat.
He didn't miss much, whether he merely glanced at a lane-side, or
whether he looked deep into the tormented mind of Hamlet or
of King Lear.

MOST of Shakespeare's flowers belong to the spring; I suppose
they are the most precious for all of us, those few-and-far-between
first-comers at hedgeroot or wood-corner, the snowdrop, the
primrose, the celandine, the sloe like a very thin sprinkling of snow
on black twigs, the marsh marigold, the wild daffodil, the wood
anemone. They are the flowers which made the most impression
on us when we were children, when we first became aware of
flowers at our feet. I can still remember my first celandine and
my delighted surprise at its yellow glossiness; the smell and softness
of the first cowslip bell; the first buttercup held up to somebody's
chin on a sunny day with a " Do you like butter? "—and you did
like butter if the golden reflection showed on your skin. We
looked at flowers more closely then. We saw the pink flush on the
underside of the daisy-floret, whereas to-day, for most of us, it's
just a white star studding the lawn.

We used to call the wild daffodils Affies, and we bicycled across
the Severn into the red-sandstone country where they grew (John
Masefield's *Daffodil Fields*) and came back with huge bunches which
we hawked round the neighbours at a few pence for a sticky double-
handful. The gypsies, who were on the move from their winter-
quarters, did likewise but sold smaller bunches at a higher price.

When the March wind flutters these daffodils they seem to
come alive, and you might almost suppose them to be winged

things, anchored only by their fragile stems to the ground. How stolid by comparison are the marsh marigolds (which we called kingcups and which were Shakespeare's ' cuckoo-buds of golden hue '). They have a pleasing buxomness, and look aggressively healthy, like farmers' daughters in old prints. What pale waifs beside them are the wood anemones, the delicate windflowers, of which Gerard the herbalist wrote so sweetly:

" It hath small leaves very much snipt or jagged, among which rises up a stalke bare or naked almost to the top; and at the top of the stalke cometh forth a faire and beautiful floure which never doth open itself but when the wind do blow."

How EVOCATIVE a thing is a flower! I shall never see a yellow crocus standing against brown earth like a candle burning in a still air but I shall remember Saint James's Park on an early March morning in 1944. I had spent three months in the Admiralty, working very hard and scarcely ever seeing the sun. I blinked like an owl in daylight as I walked through the park to Norfolk House, which was then the naval headquarters for the coming Invasion. There were regiments of crocuses, a blackbird was singing, the ducks were flirting and preening themselves, and a picnicking group of Waafs in their shirt-sleeves were flirting and preening themselves too. The spring looked different, though, when I walked back an hour later. In that hour I had learned the whole Allied plan for the invasion of Normandy. That intelligence—and the horrid responsibility of *knowing*—felt like a heavy load as I went back towards my office through the crocus-companies all drawn up on parade. I was at once excited by the magnitude of the secret and envious of the untroubled Waafs to whom nobody had said: " You have got to be told certain things and from now until we set sail you, and a few hundred others, carry our whole safety in your heads. . . ."

Bluebells for me are invasion-flowers too. Our headquarters at Southwick House, looking down on Portsmouth, had a big wildish garden, with streams and a pond, shrubberies and coppice. I shall never forget the bluebells there on still and shining days at the end of May—days when the nations, and the very elements too, seemed to be holding their breath. I swear they were bluer than any bluebells anywhere! And the buttercups in the field beyond the gardens were more golden; the hawthorn made a creamier snow-drift; the little stitchwort in the hedgerow was a purer white than I had ever seen before. That was on the day before we left to join the biggest Armada mankind has ever launched into a huge hazard; and I for one shall never look upon the little flowers so eagerly, so hungrily almost, nor see them again so bright and clear—

ENGLAND, 1944

It was a season to match our spendthrift mood.
The banners were hung out on thorn and tree.
Never so many bluebells in the wood
That time when all ways led towards the sea.

And lo, on Hampshire hill and Devon combe
The beacons spoke to friend and enemy.
The call to arms was lit on gorse and broom
That time when all hills ran towards the sea.

The Cuckoo's Stay

I never saw the lanes look lovelier.
The English earth was prodigal as we,
Sparing no umbelled flower nor crucifer
That time when all lanes led towards the sea.

As one whose heart breaks, yet for holiday
Decks herself out, none should be fine as she,
England made merry as we marched away
That time when all her sons marched to the sea.

III

ALMOST every angler has a favourite stream, and a favourite reach in that stream, and perhaps a favourite willow-tree over-hanging that reach. My stream is on the Cotswolds, my reach is where it bends in the shape of a longbow, my willow-tree grows aslant and leans far over the water like poor Ophelia's. There is no tree lovelier than the willow, though its very name is sad, say it aloud to yourself, but softly, and it is like an unrequited lover's sigh! This the makers of songs well know. O willow waly! they cry; and

> *All around my hat*
> *I wear the green willow,*
> *All around my hat*
> *For a twelve-months and a day;*
> *And if anyone shall ask me*
> *The reason of my sorrow,*
> *I will tell them that my true love's gone*
> *Far, far away!*

But not all willows weep. Some, dressed in Lincoln-green in the late spring, have the lightness and the grace of young maiden-hood; others, old ones, at winter twilight are like ancient hags, witch-like, malevolent, holding up crooked arms in supplication, warning, despair. No other tree, I think, has so many moods. I love it, and delight in its infinite variety, though it hasn't the grandeur of the great Forest trees. The botanists have differen-tiated and named with long names an immense number of species and subspecies; but this seems to me an unremarkable achievement, for the poets can differentiate ten thousand. No willow is like another willow. The other day I came across a row of very old ones, so ancient that their trunks had split, and some of them were bifurcated and seemed to stand upon two legs like gnarled old men, and some even had three legs like Triffids. But somehow or other their roots survived and got some sustenance from the soil; and in turn they gave sustenance to other plants and trees which had

seeded themselves in the leaf mould and rotting wood which filled some of the space between the splits in the trunks. Miniature gardens and indeed miniature shrubberies grew there: willow herb, loosestrife, groundsel, dog-rose, sycamore, hawthorn, privet, even little nut-bushes, growing almost as if they had been grafted there, out of the tops of the trunks of those ancient willow-trees!

As an amateur naturalist I love willows not only for themselves but for their parasites. Exciting caterpillars inhabit them. In the rotten wood you find the big hideous grubs of the goatmoth, which burrows in the wood and chews it into sawdust, living there for more than two years before it turns into a great grey moth. Goatmoth caterpillars smell like goats; it is possible, when you stand to windward of a goat-infested willow-stump, to identify them by their smell.

Then there are puss-moth caterpillars, and eyed hawks, and the caterpillars of red underwings which when they turn into moths always remind me of old women with red flannel petticoats; for their forewings are drab, brown and grey, and it is only when they lift them that you suddenly see the black-hemmed bright scarlet of the hindwings underneath.

MY FAVOURITE WILLOW, the one beside the Cotswold trout stream, has a half-submerged bough which serves as a platform for the water-rats, that swim out to it from the bank. Late one evening I watched two of them, which I think were a pair, swim to the branch together, climb on to it, and play there prettily and affectionately until suddenly and for no apparent reason they both lost their tempers and fought fiercely until they both fell in. Water-voles are liable to such little paddies, but they soon get over them, and before long the pair had returned to their branch and sat side by side preening their whiskers, so close to me that I could have touched them with the tip of my rod.

A VERY strange little creature inhabits this Cotswold stream. It carries its skeleton outside its body, its jaws outside its mouth, and its stomach in its head. It has white blood, and prefers to swim backwards rather than forwards. If it loses a limb, it gradually grows a new one. Its stomach contains two small stones (used in crushing its food) which old wives and herbalists used to set great store by, regarding them as a magical cure for a great many ills; but in fact they consist simply of carbonate of lime, or chalk.

This little monster is called the crayfish. It is related to the lobster, and the *langouste* of Southern France, and is quite as good to eat. We catch it either by wading in the stream and ' groping ' for it under stones or under tree-roots or in water-rats' holes; or by tying some bait, such as rabbits' innards, bits of liver, meat or fish into a faggot made of well-branched twigs of hawthorn. We tie a piece of string to the faggot and cast it out in a suitable place; and in fifteen minutes or so we draw it slowly in and are often rewarded with a haul of three or four crayfish caught up among the twigs. A very old book on local natural history recommends most strangely " A soldier's old scarlet jacket is a most attractive and catching bait ", but I don't know why this should be nor whether indeed the eyes of the crayfish can distinguish colours at all.

The biggest I have ever seen was about six and a half inches long; but the average size is much smaller. They are olive in colour, dark on top, light underneath, and, like lobsters, go red when you boil them. They taste much the same as lobsters, or those ' Dublin bay prawns ' which are so delicious and which a friend once described to me, while they lay on the dish before him, as looking like " El Greco saints in ecstasy "; indeed they have the same translucent, skeletal and agonised air.

You can keep crayfish in an aquarium (though I have never done so myself) where according to an old naturalist, Mr. Edwin Burgh of Gloucestershire, " they are by no means a jovial crew and maintain a sullen and reserved demeanour." He describes their feeding habits as follows:

" When they were fed the big one was always the first to seize the food; he invariably did this with the left forceps, holding it at arms' length, then bringing it to his mouth and nibbling for a few minutes, then again holding it out and apparently admiring it. This performance would be continued for nearly an hour, at the end of which he would slowly crawl to his rest, taking the remnants of the meal with him. . . .

" Their principal food consisted of brandlings, gilt-tails, green peas (which they did not care much about), boiled potato, liver, bits of fish, salmon roe and trout spawn, which they preferred to anything else."

This suggests that the crayfish may do a certain amount of harm in trout-streams; it is certainly in the clear Cotswold trout-streams, such as the Colne, that we find them most plentiful. But the trout get their own back, for they feed freely on the young crayfish, when they are soft and have not yet grown their shells. Thus the two organisms co-exist, if not happily at least to their mutual benefit—and to ours; for we who live so far from the sea and have no easy harvest of crabs, lobsters and prawns almost at our doorsteps can do with a dish of these crustaceans now and then, and it is fun to spend an evening catching them (for they feed best at night) with the baited hawthorn bough or even, I suppose—if we could obtain it!—" the soldier's old scarlet jacket" discarded long ago by Coldstream or Grenadier.

IV

Not far from my Cotswold chalk-stream is a bank where the wild thyme blows; and among the wild thyme there survives a colony of Large Blues.

The Large Blue is one of the rarest and certainly the most precarious of our native butterflies. Its colonies are small and scattered, and sometimes occupy an area of less than an acre; so the butterfly is very difficult to find (unless you know exactly where to look), but when found it is very liable to extermination by greedy or commercial collectors. For there *is* a commerce in these rarities: I believe that specimens of the Large Blue will fetch 5s. to 10s. each among the dealers in such things. Therefore those few of us who know the Cotswold haunts of this butterfly take care to keep our secret.

One colony, which had been discovered by the semi-professional collectors, was saved by the action of a public-spirited local entomologist who spent three or four days catching the butterflies, rubbing the scales off their wings, and letting them go. This made them worthless to the collectors, who arrived subsequently, but did the butterflies no harm, so that they mated and laid their eggs and the colony survives to this day.

The rarity of the butterfly is due to a peculiarity in its life-history. The eggs are laid upon the thyme, and the little caterpillar feeds on its blossoms from July until early autumn; so the first requisite for a colony of Large Blues is a good patch of thyme. But after its third moult the caterpillar wanders away from its food plant and allows itself to be discovered by a particular kind of ant, which seizes it in its jaws and bears it off to the brood chamber of the ant-hill.

The ant does not, however, devour the caterpillar. It is too valuable to be eaten; for it exudes from a gland in its body a kind of sweet liquid which is to the ant as honeydew or indeed ambrosia. Its captors ' milk ' it two or three times a day; and to keep it alive they feed it on their own offspring. Upon this sacrificial fare the caterpillar waxes fat and being confined in darkness becomes very unlike a butterfly-caterpillar, but in the nature of a maggot: a fat, fleshy-white grub.

When winter comes it goes to sleep, and in the warm ant-hill hibernates till spring. Wakening in April or May, it is fattened once again upon the ant grubs (which are erroneously called ' ants-eggs ' and are also appreciated by tame gold-fish) and so in the course of time changes to a chrysalis. Out of this chrysalis in July there emerges what I think is the loveliest of all our British butterflies; and having found its way by a complexity of corridors out of the ant-hill and into the sunshine, it takes wing and flies in the sun.

The association, for their mutual benefit, of the caterpillar and the ant, is called Simbiosis, which is defined as ' a non-parasitic partnership between two organisms '. How in the course of evolution this association arose can only be guessed at; and we do not know how many million years ago it began. But obviously at some stage (and possibly by some accident) the butterfly and the ant discovered the mutual advantages of the association and adapted themselves to it. From the butterfly's point of view, the possibility of doom lies in the affair; for it has now adapted itself so completely to the relationship that *it could not exist without the ant*. Its caterpillar could not survive the winter outside the ant-hill, nor in all probability could the caterpillar's metabolism continue to deal with a diet of wild thyme *after* the third moult: it must feed on ant-grubs or die. The ant, on the other hand, is not dependent on the butterfly. The caterpillar-milk is a luxury to it, not a necessity.

So you see how precarious is the Large Blue's hold upon survival.

It must have wild thyme, it must have the ant, and one without the other is useless to it. It may be that there are not many places in Cornwall or on Cotswold where the conditions are just right; and if the County Agricultural Committee should choose to direct a farmer to plough up a particular field this *may* result in the extinction of yet another colony. Meanwhile other small or unlucky colonies may be wiped out by the over-enthusiasm of collectors, a wet, cold season, or the use of a new fertiliser or weed-killer on the land; or these conditions may so tip the balance against them that they will soon die out of their own accord.

For my part I should be very surprised if there are any Large Blues to be found in Britain, outside collections, in 50 years' time; which is the reason, I suppose, why people are prepared to pay several shillings for specimens and so unthinkingly hasten the process of extinction.

It is surprising how few of our native butterflies have been made extinct by man's activities. The great Purple Emperor still flies in his imperial fashion among the treetops of our remaining highwoods, and the Black Hairstreak holds out here and there. Swallowtails are still pretty common on the Norfolk Broads. The Black-veined White died out of its own accord early in this century; and although

143

the English Large Copper is extinct in the Fens an allied Dutch species was brought over by some butterfly enthusiast; one or two colonies of this insect still thrive in Cambridgeshire. Another very pretty little continental butterfly called *Arashnia levana* was introduced into the Forest of Dean in 1912, where it not only survived but increased in numbers. It might to-day be as familiar as our native tortoiseshells, peacocks and red admirals, but for the action of a serious and puritanical entomologist who held the strange view that there was something improper, and even immoral, in the introduction of a foreign species into Britain. He set himself the task of destroying the two colonies of this charming butterfly; and within a few years he personally slaughtered the lot. It seems to me a monstrous thing to do; but if any landlord possessing woods, leisure, and the spirit of experiment cares to undo the deed all he has to do is to import from north-east France, at the cost of a few pounds, some thousand or two caterpillars of *levana* in the proper season and put them down upon some clumps of stinging-nettle. In ten years time he will probably be rewarded by seeing the speckled red-and-brown, white-banded butterflies sitting in number on the thistle-heads. But there is no certainty, for the factors which make for survival are complex and interrelated, and as yet we know very little about them.

For instance, somebody had the bright idea of introducing the Cinnabar moth into New Zealand; for New Zealand was suffering from a great infestation of the common weed called ragwort, which had probably found its way there as an accidental adulteration of some imported grass-seed. Now the caterpillars of the Cinnabar moth feed greedily upon ragwort; and in Britain they are so plentiful that they act as an important control of this tiresome weed. A few score of full-fed Cinnabars will strip a patch of ragwort of its leaves in a few days, and you may then see them hanging miserably to the bare stems,—rather pretty caterpillars with alternate black and orange rings. This striking football-jersey appearance seems to make the birds shy of them. It is the same ' warning coloration ' which wasps have. The birds leave them alone, and the Cinnabar moth, with its scarlet hind-wings, is one of our commoner insects.

So Mr. Newman, the ' butterfly farmer' of Bexley, Kent, was commissioned to provide 60,000 chrysalises of the Cinnabar moth and send them off to New Zealand, and these were put down among the vast tracts of ragwort. They hatched into moths which duly laid their eggs, the caterpillars fell upon the ragwort-leaves with enthusiasm, and for a time it looked as if the ingenious experiment was going to succeed. It was frustrated by the New Zealand birds. It seems that the ' warning colours' which frightened our British birds meant nothing in New Zealand. Possibly in the Antipodes the nauseous, distasteful, and dangerous insects wear different colours for their self-protection. At any rate the finches of New Zealand were quick to learn that the black-and-orange football jerseys signified a succulent meal; they fed fat upon the Cinnabar caterpillars; and they wiped them out as completely as the late Mr. Farn, that indignant butterfly-collector, wiped out the colonies of *Arashnia levana* in the Forest of Dean. The ragwort in New Zealand continued to spread, until the new hormone weed-killers, far more destructive than nature's own remedy, succeeded where the caterpillars had failed.

V

THERE ARE, I think, 2,299 different sorts of butterflies and moths to be found in Britain; a number of the species have not been known to breed here, so we shan't be far wrong if we say there are about 2,250 different sorts of caterpillars. However, an old gardener I know holds that there are only two sorts: PILLYGRUBS and CANKERWORMS. The Pillygrubs are hairy, the Cankerworms are smooth. I don't know why he troubles thus to differentiate them; for he squashes both sorts impartially with a very large boot.

I have liked caterpillars ever since, as a boy of seven, I kept my first cage-full of puss-moths. These would be cankerworms according to the old gardener's classification. They are quaint things with baboon-like faces and scarlet twin tails called flagellae because they are like little whips. In colour they are a delicious lime-green with a velvety purplish saddle across the back. They feed on sallow, and when I was at school there was a sallow bush which we had to pass every Sunday on our way to church. One Sunday it was simply swarming with pusses (which incidentally were saleable for five sweets apiece); so possessing no box in which to confine them I put them loose in my pockets and continued upon my way. As I knelt in church I felt a tickle at the back of my neck; and soon I heard the first giggle behind me. There were puss caterpillars crawling all over me, and before long the whole school was giggling while I buried my face in the English Hymnal, which book in its green-cloth binding I have ever since associated with pusses.

Being the horrid little boy I was, it occurred to me to make a corner in caterpillars; and like a cunning capitalist I bought up, very secretly, all the puss-moth catties in the school. When I owned the lot, or nearly the lot, I was in a position to put up the price. I had to be careful not to flood the market; so I sold just a few at a time, for about 15 sweets each. This gave me great power, which I exercised despotically. Then, suddenly, somebody discovered a sallow-bush which provided a new, prolific source of pusses. The price fell. I became very poor, and very unpopular.

HAWK-MOTH caterpillars were worth even more than pusses, and a Death's Head Hawk was beyond price. This moth (the biggest in Britain) possesses a squeak,—quite a loud one, though nobody seems quite sure how it produces it. Two learned French entomologists tried to find out. M. Lorey said the noise came from the abdomen; M. Duponchel said that was nonsense because he'd heard it when the abdomen was cut off. Et moi, retorted M. Lorey, I have heard it when the head was cut off. So we can conclude nothing from this controversy save that perhaps we should all squeak if we were subjected to the insatiable curiosity of French scientists.

OTHER favourite caterpillars of our schooldays were woolly-bears (which turn into beautiful tiger-moths) and drinkers, brown furry caterpillars which later produce big brown moths. They are so called because they sip the drops of rain or dew which they find upon the grass. However, they were not to be compared with the pusses, which when teased would spit formic acid at you and alas were therefore frequently teased. Moreover the pusses made fancy cocoons out of any material you cared to give them— bits of coloured paper, rag, glass beads or bits of string. In their natural state, of course, they have to be content with fragments of chewed-up bark which they mix with gummy saliva to make a cocoon so hard that you could hardly break it with a hammer. But Nature, all providing, supplies the chrysalis with a private reservoir of caustic potash which it ejects at the appropriate moment, so softening the cocoon from the inside, and allowing the perfect moth to emerge.

All this I learned when I was ten; but I also learned, through trading caterpillars for sweets, some of the elementary principles of high finance. They, however, seem to have been little use to me; for I have never since those days failed to buy anything I needed —from a car to a house—at the very top of the market nor to sell, usually out of hard necessity, at the precise moment when the market reached its nadir.

THE MOST exciting caterpillars I ever possessed were given to me, only last summer, by a small boy who'd swopped a book about space-travel for them with another small boy who'd bought them from a natural history dealer for a shilling apiece. They were caterpillars of the Indian Moon-Moth. They fed upon walnut-leaves, and my young friend couldn't find any walnut growing near his home. He tired of going for long bicycle-rides in search of walnut, and cricket had taken the place of caterpillars as the chief interest of his life, so I became the owner of the jamjar with the desiccated walnut-leaves and the two ravenous caterpillars inside it. To make up for their long hunger I fed them fresh food every day until they were as fat as Strasbourg geese, and in due course they made themselves large silken cocoons and turned into chrysalises. Then one evening a male Moon-Moth hatched out. It was the most exquisite winged creature I had ever seen. Its colour was a kind of luminescent green, a very pale green that had a tinge of acid yellow in it. You must think of a lime-green Chinese lantern, paper thin, hanging in a dark garden with the light shining through it! There were small transparent half-moons, edged with brown and yellow, in the centre of each wing; the hind wings bore long green ' tails '—two inches long and gracefully tapered—which shaded into yellow towards their tips. The body of the moth was fluffy and buff-coloured, and upon its head it bore antennae toothed like tiny combs.

It was, as I say, the most exquisite winged thing in all my

experience, until a female hatched the following night and she, its predestined mate, was both larger and lovelier. Now I had never seen the mating-flight of these Moon-Moths, so on an evening scented with tobacco-flower, and hushed, and appropriately moon-lit, I took them both into the garden, he perched upon my right hand, she upon my left, and offered them as it were to Selene.

She was at her fullest, high in the sky and silvery. She shone upon the green wings of the moths and changed them to some colour between green and silver for which there is no name; mermaids' tails may be of that colour, or Neptune's trident; who knows? Gently, gently the wings vibrated, but the moths were in no hurry to leave their perch upon my hands. They moon-bathed, as we do bask in the sun.

I stood still, waiting for the moment when they would surely leave me. The moon put poetry into my head, and I thought of poor Cleopatra's agonised cry when her Antony was dead: " Nothing left remarkable Beneath the visiting moon." It occurred to me that in a century or so there may, for our grandchildren, be nothing left remarkable *upon* the visiting moon. They will stand among those jagged craters and look about them at the dead, dead landscape upon which nothing ever stirs: the bare mountains, the huge chasms, the cold empty desert ghostly-grey in the light re-flected upon it by our earth, a greater moon than ever you and I will gaze upon. And far away earth may look to them as beau-tiful, as mysterious, as the moon did to me when I stood in the midnight garden with the moth-wings pulsing on my palm.

And now Nature working within them chose for them their hour. It was he who left me first, the little male. (I say little, but his wing-span was three inches at least; hers must have been between four and five.) He rose as lightly as thistledown in an up-current on a hot day, and then she was with him, then she was above him, and ascending more quickly than he, in widening spirals which he followed, a little beneath her, but always matching his course to hers.

This was the mating-flight. It was strange and wonderful; and the moths were so big, and the moon was so bright, that I could watch it for thirty seconds or so, staring up into the sky.

Up, up they went. Would they mate upon the wing or fall to earth when wings and ecstasy could bear them no higher? I did not know. They vanished from my view; and I could almost imagine they had fled to the moon, that gave them her name and whose crescent symbols they bore upon their wings.

But alas no. They are of the earth, as you and I. And our grandsons, the space-men, though they stand upon the very moon-mountains themselves, will not find there anything so strange nor anything half so lovely as those Moon-Moths of mine which hatched in the schoolboy's jamjar, and perched for a little while upon my outstretched hand.

VI

MY GOOSEBERRY-BUSHES are being stripped of their leaves by a kind of caterpillar that is neither Pillygrub nor Cankerworm, but is semi-transparent, flaccid, beige-coloured, and obscene. This is the larva of the sawfly, and it fills me with such dismay that even as I spray the gooseberry-bushes to get rid of it I find it necessary to avert my head. The good Sir Thomas Browne would see God's handiwork in it, but he is a better man than I shall ever be. He wrote, in 1640: " I cannot start at the presence of a serpent, scorpion, lizard or salamander. I find in me no desire to take up a stone to destroy them. I feel not in myself those common antipathies that I can discover in others." For him, wise man, good physician, humble lover of all created things, there was no deformity but in monstrosity. " I cannot tell by what logic we call a toad, a bear, or an elephant ugly, they being created in those outward shapes and figures which best express those actions of their inward forms."

Most of us, however, are less fortunate than Sir Thomas Browne; we suffer from certain ' common antipathies '—against snails, slugs, caterpillars, and what not. The strange thing is that we do not share the *same* antipathies. For example, I like snakes; I do not mind handling them; yet I detest eels, and will not touch one if I can help it. Because the latter is cold and slimy? Yet I feel no reluctance to handle other fish. It is inexplicable. Caterpillars (other than those of the sawfly) enchant me; I let them crawl over my hand. But if *Limax*, the big black slug, or worse still the big brown spotted slug whose proper name I know not, were to crawl over my hand I should be sick. I adore oysters; but I'd be hard put to it to eat a snail. And so on.

Generally speaking I think it is the cold, clammy, smooth, serpentine thing that I abhor. But other people possess a horror, incomprehensible to me, of fur and feather. My wife, intrepid about caterpillars, is terrified of a fluttering bird. Mice send some women into hysterics; and most women are unaccountably frightened of bats. There is no arguing about these antipathies; we are made so, and there's an end of it. I don't know if we could conquer our revulsions; possibly we could—because I once knew a man who was mad on fishing but could not bring himself to put a worm on his hook. So he employed his poor wife to carry out this humble task. One day, growing old, she suddenly went on strike. Never again, she said; it was not the worms only, but the weather, and the river-damp which got into her bones, and the sheer boredom which she'd already put up with for too long. But did the man therefore give up fishing? He did not. Thereafter he put on his own worms.

The counterpart of that story concerns an encounter I had with a middle-aged woman who was herself devoted to angling. I found her sitting by the river putting together her tackle. Upon her hook unmoved by any kind of revulsion she threaded a fat lobworm. To the top of her rod she had fixed a small ingenious bell. Before long this bell began to tinkle. Rousing herself at the sound she pulled out a little eel. Seizing it with her bare hand she declared crossly " Oh, it's swallowed the hook " and proceeded to cut its head off with a penknife while I watched her with a curious mixture of horror, nausea and respect. Then she wiped the penknife and employed it to cut slices out of a pork-pie.

However, when I returned by the same path later that afternoon I discovered that this remarkable woman who had no fear of worms and eels nevertheless possessed her Achilles' heel. She was besieged by a small herd of heifers of which she was simply terrified and which, as she called out to me for help, she insisted were bulls.

She was standing in her gumboots about two yards out in the river, defending herself with the frail lance represented by her fishing-rod. From this predicament I rescued her, and when I had driven away the heifers she sat down, intrepid once more, to thread upon her hook another wriggling worm.

VII

COUNTRYMEN set store by anniversaries; especially I think anniversaries of disaster. Every 5th of June in the Swan bar at Elmbury somebody is "minded" of the great flood of 1924.

It was not only the worst flood we remember, but the swiftest. I was playing cricket on the Swilgate Meadow at 3.30 on the Saturday afternoon; a downpour sent us scurrying into the pavilion. We had tea early on the chance that we'd be able to resume the game later. We said we'd look at the pitch at 5. But at 5 we couldn't see the pitch; the Swilgate Brook in a turbulent brown flood had come tearing over it. By 6.30 the pavilion was flooded. Next day Severn and Avon began to come up so fast that astonished old men, leaning upon bridges as old men do on Sunday mornings, brought out turnip watches to measure the rate of the rise: inches to the half hour.

Summer floods, of course, are rare and therefore catastrophic. They ruin the crops and catch the farmers' stock in the river meadows. Nobody is prepared for them. This flood soon began to bring down with it not only debris but a strange harvest from the river's upper reaches. Haycocks, half submerged like ice-bergs; empty boats, torn from light summer moorings; drowned cattle, sheep and pigs; a carthorse, swimming, which someone skilfully lassoed and dragged ashore. There was a fowlhouse with a barnyard cockerel sitting on top of it. It bumped against the supports of King John's Bridge, then tore through one of the arches, whizzing round and round like a teetotum. The rooster looked bewildered, fluttered his wings hopelessly, and crowed as if he cried "Ahoy!"

to the watchers on the next bridge downstream. The old men gave him a cheer.

On Pitchcroft Meadow, at Worcester, all had been prepared for the Three Counties' Agricultural Show. Severn flowing at a good seven knots brought down the stands and tent-poles and sheds and what-not to Elmbury; the townspeople became beach-combers and longshoremen and ran along the edge of the flood picking up enough sound timber to build themselves punts and chicken-coops and potting-sheds and rabbit-hutches; to keep them busy carpentering for years to come. Some enterprising fellows took out their own boats on the river and salvaged material worth many pounds. But it was hard work, and even dangerous, so three of our local spivs and scroungers, whom I have nicknamed elsewhere Pistol, Bardolph and Nym, discovered an easier way of making a little fortune to be squandered in the Black Bear, the White Bear, the Shakespeare and the George. They acquired, somehow, an old horse, shoulder-shotten, spavined, gone in the wind, and harnessed it to a set of chains and traces. Bardolph and Nym had charge of the horse, and stood at the edge of the flood where it ran across the Worcester road, calling out to each successive motorist:

" Tow you through for five bob, Mister! "

Five bob was a lot of money in those days: it represented, for the motorist, about five gallons of petrol; for Pistol, Bardolph and Nym more than seven gallons of rough cider. So while the motorist hesitated, or perhaps tried to haggle with the scroungers, along came Pistol shaking his fist at his pals.

" Don't 'ee believe 'em, Mister! Thee can get through easy. 'Tis only about 18 inches in the middle. They'm robbers. Don't 'ee have no truck."

So the motorist would decide to risk it. Bardolph and Nym would chorus:

" If thee gets stuck, then, don't-ee holler for us to pull 'ee out! "

But it was more than three feet in the middle. At last the car's engine gave a final despairing cough, and the self-starter whirred in vain. Out plodded Bardolph and Nym in their seaboots,

Bardolph pulling the reluctant Dobbin by the head, Nym bela-bouring it from behind.

" What did us tell 'ee, Mister?   But us couldn't leave 'ee out here to get thy feet wet.   Pull 'ee out for half a quid! "

Pistol took his commission, of course, upon the extra five bob. I dare say the scoundrels " earned " five or ten pounds apiece during the three or four days while the flood lasted.   They were drunk for as many weeks afterwards.

The flood left a stinking residue behind it.   The hay and the unmown grass rotted in the fields.   There were no buttercups on Elmbury Ham that year, no huddle of ricks in the yard by the Old Mill.   The silt lay three inches deep in Elmbury's cellars, and for weeks afterwards, on every sunny day, you saw the cottagers putting out their pathetic sticks of furniture to dry.   The queer musty smell of the flood was in our nostrils for ages; and the old men, each summer, will smell it again in memory.   June, 1924: when Elmbury was an island, and punts plied in the streets, and men brought out their penknives and made little marks in the brick or stone of their houses, marks which you can still find if you look for them, to record for their sons and their grandsons the topmost limit of that memorable flood.

The Parish Register of a village farther up the Avon tells of an even greater summer flood than ours.   On the 18th of July, 1588, when from Cornwall to Sussex every manjack was looking to his weapons and turning his eyes towards the sea, the folks who lived in the heart of England were getting in their hay; and this peaceful task probably seemed to the farmers of greater immediate impor-tance than repelling an Armada, for the weather was breaking, there were black clouds piling up on the horizon and rumbles of thunder in the distance.   Most fittingly, upon that day, there was an electric feeling in the air.

Now in Hillborough Meadow, not far below Stratford—they called it Haunted Hillboro' in an old rhyme—a young woman named Miss Sale was pitching the hay into cocks, and doubtless doing so in a great hurry, for up north, towards Warwick, the storm had already broken. So she worked fast, but not fast enough, for the Avon began to come down in a thick brown flood and shortly it burst its banks at Hillborough and broke into the big meadow, swirling among the haycocks, sweeping through the swathes. Upstream, ever since eight o'clock in the morning the great summer flood had spread destruction far and wide. According to the Parish Register of Welford-on-Avon, whose Clerk had a lively pen, " Old Father Porter, being then 105 years of age, never knew it so high by a yard and a half. Dwelling in the mill-house he, in former times, knew it under his bed, but this flood was a yard and a half in the house, and came in so sudden that John Perry's wife was so amazed that she sate still till she was almost drowned, and was wellnigh beside herself, and so far amiss that she did not know her own child when it was brought to her. . . . (The flood) brake down Grange Mill, the crack thereof was heard at Holditch. It brake up sundry houses in Warwick Town, and carried away their bread, beef, cheese, butter, pots, pans, and provisions, and took away ten carts out of one town, and three wains, with the furniture of Thomas Lucy, and brake both ends of Stratford Bridge."

Shakespeare, sad to say, did not witness this awesome spectacle; almost certainly, he had gone up to London two years before : but doubtless some of his Stratford friends wrote him accounts of it, and he was probably delighted to hear that it had taken away Thomas Lucy's furniture—if this was the same Thomas Lucy of Charlecote whom he later pilloried as Mr. Justice Shallow.

However, that is by the way; for we are concerned with the fortunes of Miss Sale, who was already getting her feet wet in Hillborough Meadow. She was more resourceful than the supine Mrs. Perry, " wellnigh beside herself " in Father Porter's mill-house; so she jumped up on to her haycock and sat there, like Miss Muffet upon her tuffet, while the flood-waters raced past. But alas, the flood deepened; and soon, in the words of Welford's Parish Clerk, " she had no shift but to get upon the top of the haycock, and was carried thereupon by the water a quarter of a mile wellnigh."

It must have been a perilous voyage: for the haycock, being at first full of air-bubbles, would have floated high out of the water, with Miss Sale, waving her pitchfork and hollering pitifully, perched upon its summit. But as the hay became sodden it doubtless began to submerge; and soon it was floating like an iceberg, with three quarters of its bulk under water; and Miss Sale's feet were getting wet again. At this juncture there came rescuers in a boat; and they pursued Miss Sale downstream until she came to " the very last bank " (presumably below that point the river had spilled out like an inland sea, and indeed it may have appeared to Miss Sale that the steep Atlantic wave lay before her). She was now, however, rescued; but her troubles were by no means at an end, for the boat nearly foundered and " all in it were like to be drowned " but that " another boat coming rescued them soon." So Miss Sale went home to dry clothes and perhaps an egg-noggin to warm her, while the ravaging flood raced on towards Evesham and Elmbury.

Next day, from the Lizard in Cornwall, a sharp-eyed coast-guard spied the masts of the invaders pricking the horizon like a little forest growing up there; Sir Francis Drake and Lord Howard of Effingham put to sea; and the bonfires were blazing and the church bells were ringing all over England. Miss Sale, from her home at Grafton, may have seen the pinpoints of light appearing like new stars low in the sky; on Cleeve Cloud, on Winchcombe, on Brensham Hill. All the way up the Channel, as the running fight went on and the fireships crackled and the cannon thundered and the great galleons foundered, the sailors of England and Spain were clinging to masts and spars, swimming in the turbulent sea, drowning by the score. For the storm that was nearly the end of Miss Sale had proved to be Drake's ally, and had beaten great Philip of Spain. Miss Sale, however, probably knew nothing of this. She heard the church bells ringing and her thankful heart echoed them. She too had sailed upon the unpathed waters; but her voyage was over and she had come safe to port.

OF COURSE these visitations are rare. For most of the time our summer Avon meanders, and is clear enough for a boy's sharp eye to spot the striped perch lazily swimming among the water-lily stems—as Shakespeare's eye must have spotted them when he leaned on the bridge at Stratford and dreamed of the Nile and Cleopatra's painted barge. Tawny-finned fishes! He was surely an angler; no boy brought up on Avonside could be otherwise. "My bended hook shall pierce their slimy jaws". Elizabethan literature is full

of references to fishing, which was already a popular sport. In Beaumont and Fletcher there are some quaint lines:

> *And when the weather*
> *Serves to angle in the brook,*
> *I will bring you a silver hook*
> *With a line of finest silk*
> *And a rod as white as milk.*

As white as milk? Possibly Messrs. Beaumont and Fletcher angled as schoolboys do, with a willow-wand stripped of its bark.

John Dennys, an Elizabethan gentleman who lived in Gloucestershire, wrote practical instructions regarding the art of angling in rather bad verse; even his description of a hook was matched to a classical reference:

> *That hooke I love that is encompast round*
> *Like to the print that Pegasus did make*
> *With hornéd hoof upon Thessalian ground. . . .*

He gives an amusing and somewhat puzzling list of fish which may be caught upon the worm:

> *And with this bait hath often taken been*
> *The Salmon fair, of River fish the best;*
> *The Shad that in the Spring time cometh in,*
> *The Suant swift that is not set by least,—*

(What on earth is a Suant? The nearest guess I can make is a Sea Trout, which the Welsh call Sewin. And what is—)

> *The Bocher sweet, the pleasant Flounder thin,*
> *The Peale, the Tweate, the Batling and the rest*
> *With many more that in the deep doe lye*
> *Of Avon, Uske, of Severn and of Wye.*

I have long fished those rivers, but I have never as far as I know caught a sweet Bocher or a Batling. The Tweate is what we nowadays call the Twaite; the Peale is another name for the sea-trout, very rare in our West Midland rivers, though common of course in Scotland, the North of England, and Wales.

WILLIAM BROWNE (1616) knew his fishes. He wrote of " the ever-nibbling roach " and what angler will not recognise a fellow-angler from that single phrase? He also wrote of " The foolish gudgeon quickly caught." John Dennys, surprisingly, refers to " the whole-some Ruffe "—a little spiny fish, called Daddy-Ruffe or Pope, which nowadays we never think of eating; he warns against Barbel, as do all the old writers. But even eels were suspect. Says the *Regimen Sanitatis*:

Who knows not physic should be nice in choice
In eating Eels, because they hurt the voice;
Both Eels and cheese, without good store of wine
Well drunk with them, offend at any time.

Any excuse is better than none!

Not all the old poets and versifiers who wrote of angling approved of it. A queer writer called Llewellyn (1646) takes the fishes' side and declares sternly:

Fish to hooke, were the case disputed,
Are not took but executed.
Break thy rod about thy noddle,
Keep thy cork to stop thy bottle.

He particularly objects to livebaiting (" But of all men he is the cheeter Who with small fish takes the greater ") and of fishing in the close season (" Cruell man that slays on gravell Fish that great with fish doth travail "). As a humanitarian he seems to have been ahead of his time.

But the strangest discovery I ever made among the scraps and relics left behind by these little poets of angling—hardly poets perhaps, but at any rate rhymesters—was the following:

Fishing, if I, a fisher, may protest
Of pleasures is the sweetest, of sports the best;
But now the sport is marred, and wot ye why?
Fishes decrease, and fishers multiply.

We read such complaints to-day. But when was *that* written? In 1598, by one Thomas Bastard, in a book called *Chresteleros*. And in his day the whole population of Britain, at four millions, was probably less than the total number of *anglers* nowadays!

VIII

WITH my mind on the river, but tied to my desk, I have been thinking, as work and business and the Inland Revenue press hard upon me, how much I should like to be a lock-keeper. Can there really be a nicer job, in the whole of this harassing, hurrying, worrying world? There you live by the riverside in a tidy little house and the world flows past you at the leisurely pace of a river flowing softly, which is just 3½ miles an hour, walking pace, the rate at which one imagines it was meant for man's world to move, when we were created bipeds. All around your tidy little house you have a tidy little garden, lots of time to work in it during the winter, and in summer lots of passers-through who have ample time to admire it while you open the gates for them. If you are a fisherman, then you can sling out a line, whenever the mood takes you, almost from your bedroom window, you can sit and watch your float for hours, without any tiresome feeling that you are being idle and wasting time, for you are on duty as you sit there. And when at last a boat comes along you have the sense of importance which turnpike-men had on the great roads long ago. Indeed you *are* a turnpike-man, on the river highway. Leisurely you turn the wheel, leisurely you put your strong back against the arm of the lock gates, powerfully but without hurry you push. Lordly you bear towards the lock-wall that great staff which has a sort of clip on the end of it. You lower it towards the boat, and receive at the end of the long pole your tribute of 3d. or 6d.

At weekends, of course, you are pretty busy. You fill your lock with half a dozen assorted craft at a time. You look down upon their occupants with a wise, experienced, and tolerant eye. You see the fishermen in their punts setting out always so hopefully, always so despondently returning. You see the men with their girls, the steadies, the ones with different girls every Sunday. You see the children dangling limp hands in the water, the children with those little useless nets which give them such delight and which never catch anything at all, the children excitedly sniffing for the first time the queer sweet waterweedy smell of the lock. You see the bathing parties in all their different stages of sunburn, the brown, the white, the pink, the peeling. You look down upon the bosoms and the bikinis. . . . You must grow very wise, I think, very philosophical, living as a lock-keeper does, watching the human pageant go by at walking-pace, holding it up for two or three minutes, and seeing it always, as gods and angels do, from above. Occasionally, of course, the pageant produces its little comedies and its minor dramas; but they only serve to lend variety to your hours. Children fall in. You hoick them out, and become the hero of the moment. Absurd people tie up their boats to the chains of the lock and when the water falls become suspended by the bows. You rescue them from disaster. Picnic baskets fall overboard, fishing rods fall overboard, father's tin of maggots falls overboard, mother's sunhat falls overboard; you rescue all.

Even in winter, when the river runs swift and brown, you have plenty of delightful odd-jobs with which to beguile yourself. For instance, you take the half-moon tool and trim the lawn-edges, you plan the flower-beds for next season, here the geraniums, here the lobelias, here the marigolds, here the snapdragons. You plant the daff bulbs and the tulips in the borders. You paint the lock-railings and give the lifebuoy a new coat of white. Everything is ship-shape and Bristol-fashion, your life is as tidily arranged as your garden. You lean upon the arm of the lock-gate, and watch the river, and wonder what people mean by discontent!

LOCK-KEEPERS were great heroes of my childhood, when 'going through the lock' was an extra excitement added to the excitement of River Picnics; which happened about three times every summer.

Each picnic involved preparations almost on the scale of a military expedition. Sandwiches were cut, cakes were made, buns were bought, pats of butter and little jars of jam were packed in the " picnic-case " which had been somebody's wedding present, eggs were hard-boiled—" and we mustn't forget the tea, and the kettle, of course, because tea always tastes funny out of vacuum-flasks, but I wouldn't trust the river water even if it were boiled, dead cats and dogs, you know, so be sure to pack two quart bottles of tap water to go in the kettle. . . ."

All this impedimenta, plus innumerable rugs, cushions, ground-sheets, mackintoshes and umbrellas, had to be carried to the boat-house, where we had hired an enormous rowing-boat, a double-sculler, for it had to accommodate eight of us, my parents, an uncle and three aunts and my sister and myself.

My father and my uncle, shirt-sleeved and with straw boaters on their heads, had to row this galley, as it must have seemed to them, two miles upstream from Elmbury to Twyning, which was the place appointed for the picnic. The aunts sat beneath open parasols, we children dangled our hands in the water and tried to make it spurt up through our fingers in small waterspouts.

" John, don't splash. You are making your aunt quite wet. She'll catch her death. . . ."

There was always considered to be an appalling risk of catching one's death on the river. So the very hottest and stillest day was always chosen for the picnic, and my uncle and my father, both in their middle age, sweated and toiled, red-faced, nearly apo-plectic.

But at last we came to Twyning, tied up the boat, sought a suitable picnic-place (" not there, the cows have been there ") unpacked the food, laid out ground-sheets and rugs, tried to boil the kettle, swatted wasps and at last ate.

"—I always think food tastes so much *nicer* in the open air."

We children would have liked to explore the meadows, play

games, or swim; but as soon as the picnic was over it was time to go home, and there was always a sudden hurry and bustle about packing up because " it gets so chilly in the evening on the water ", and the risk of catching one's death was trebled or quadrupled after tea. So the swans were fed with the left-over sandwiches, the aunts were embarked, wrapped in rugs and " tucked in round their knees," and once again my father and my uncle endured their long martyrdom.

Dragonflies hovered, the golden water-lilies we called Brandy-bottles floated on the water, pink flowering rushes and yellow Flag-Irises stood among the reeds where fishermen watched motion-less floats.

We, too, should have liked to fish, to pick the flowers, to chase the dragonflies; but no, the evening mist was creeping up, an invisible menace, everybody was liable to catch their death at any moment, so faster and faster my father rowed, quicker and quicker came my uncle's gasps as he heaved at the sculls, the rowlocks creaked, the rippling water made music under the bow, the rowers in their haste nearly caught crabs and splashed the aunts, who were now swathed in rugs like Egyptian mummies.

"—Do please take care, you're soaking us. . . ."

" Isn't it remarkable that even on the hottest day there's always a breeze on the river? "

It was the wind, perhaps, of our own speed; the sweat was running down the rowers' faces, little pulses (curiously interesting, curiously disturbing, to us children) were throbbing in their temples, the veins in my father's arms were standing out blue and knotted. " Hurry, dear, if you can, we don't want to be caught by the mist on the water. . . ."

And there was a sense of urgency, as if the mist were a poisonous miasma, " All the infections that the sun sucks up From bogs, Fens, flats . . ."

If it overtook us we should catch our death surely. But some-how, by dint of hard rowing, we always managed to escape; and with the boat tied up at the landing stage, there was a chatter of relief, even the prim aunts felt like adventurous explorers who had returned from a dangerous journey miraculously unharmed.

". . . It was a lovely picnic, wasn't it? And we're home in quite good time, too. . . . Will you hand me the rugs out of the boat, please. We must take care to have them aired when we get home. Now hurry up, children, don't stand about, you'll be catching your death else. . . ."

IX

EVERYWHERE now, in the garden, along the lane-side, through the wood, but loudest of all, I think, among the tall bracken on the slope of the hill—everywhere there throbs and pulses a perpetual hum. For me the real quintessence of summer is this hum. It is not a bee-hum, though there are bees in it, but it is made up of the voices of innumerable little atomies whirring, buzzing, humming, pinging, most of them unseen. I have lain in the bracken on hot days and listened to it. (The smell of bruised bracken, by the way, is surely midsummer's own distinctive smell; and midsummer's distinctive sound is the voice of a very tired cuckoo calling very far away: a cuckoo that seems to say like Swinburne: I am sick of singing.) But that hum!—I have often thought that if one were an expert one could sort out the instruments in the orchestra, the fiddles of the various grasshoppers and crickets, the thin little metallic pipe of the gnats, the wood-wind of the honey-bees, the deep bass of some old bumble. This symphony of summer goes on from dawn to dusk but reaches its climax I think about mid-afternoon on a hot day. And it is not a local buzz, like that of bees at lime-flowers. It is universal, all about you. At this time of year it begins to take the place of bird-song, as one by one the singers fall silent. In fact, towards the end of June, nearly half of the birds' chorus dies away. The ones that go on singing are mostly the ones who don't mind repeating themselves: the incessant chiff-chaff, and the greenfinch that Walter de la Mare wrote of:

When summer heat hath drowsed the day
With blaze of noontide overhead
And hidden greenfinch can but say
What but a moment since it said.

And, of course, most repetitive bird of all, the corncrake. There's our true midsummer bird. His laryngal voice is inseparable from hayfields, moondaisies, the loaded wagons, the men with burnt-sienna faces and forearms, wearing the old panama hats that always come out for haymaking, pitching in the blazing sun, with their waistcoats on if they're old men—have you ever seen an old labourer shed his waistcoat? Anyhow, that's the scene the corn-crake's croak brings back to me. Nowadays the baler takes the place of the loaded wain, there are fewer hayricks and fewer corn-crakes too. But whenever I hear one I think of the swathes new-cut lying round the edge of the field, the old bone-shaking mower going round and round, and somewhere in the uncut middle, *saw-saw-saw*, like the noise we used to make with a piece of tissue-paper and a comb. The only other bird that I specially associate with high summer is the swift: low-flying squadrons of swifts screaming across a pond where as a boy I used to fish for perch. The stripes down the sides of those perch gave them a kind of camouflage as they moved to and fro in the green deeps underneath the lilypads. They looked almost transparent; they were like the ghosts of fishes. I used to lie flat on the bank and peer down into their waterweedy world; there were rudd there too, whose silvery sides took on a greenish reflection from the water-lily leaves. They were green thoughts in a green shade.

The swifts scream, the corncrake saws—there's a sort of raucousness about the birds' voices in high summer. It is a garish time. " Now do the high midsummer pomps come on,"—heavy-scented meadowsweet, loosestrife, rose-bay willow-herb, the nightshade and the henbane, the dark sinister flowers the old magicians culled from secret places at the witching hour.

The simple-gatherers must have had a busy night at midsummer; because almost all the best spells insisted that their ingredients should be collected at the very stroke of midnight. Fernseed was the great prize; if you caught it just right, it made you invisible. House-breakers and illicit lovers,—and doubtless jealous husbands too—paid high prices for it. If it didn't work, and they were betrayed in their solid substantial selves,—well, perhaps the witch's clock had been wrong, she hadn't caught it at the exact moment of midnight. . . .

When I think of these red-purple flowers of high summer, they lead me to what I am sure is my most persistent, most unfading midsummer memory. It is of a lane, dank and overgrown, with foxgloves growing up along it, and honeysuckle and wild rose in the rough hedge. The grass was long and always damp and cool against your legs. Only poachers went there, and lovers, and bughunting naturalists; and on various different occasions I was all three. If you ventured far along it the lane became a sort of alleyway between trees; so the dusk came early there, and soon the dogroses were wan white faces peering from the hedge, and the white campion was a host of smaller faces peering from the ditch, and the meadowsweet was a milky way, all blurred, and its heavy scent mixed with the heavy scent of the elder-flowers. The lane, just at dusk, was the stillest place I ever knew; so still you could hear the pale moths go by, and the breathing of some village Romeo and Juliet as they stood together under the trees: Spread your close curtain, love-performing night That runaways' eyes may wink.

And then, suddenly, the nightingale started: bubble, bubble, the sound of small stones dropping melodiously into a very deep well. And I, of course, being 18 or so, began to think like young Keats of death and immortality. . . . His poem goes to a kind of slow pulse, a throb, it matches that humming murmur of mid-summer. You can almost *hear* the heat in it.

> *The coming musk-rose, full of dewy wine,*
> *The murmurous haunt of flies on summer eves. . . .*

Queer to think that we can never smell Keats's musk-rose; for its scent has been lost, bred out of it I suppose, and it's probably true that not one of us to-day has experienced exactly what Keats did when he smelt the musk-rose and heard the nightingale.

THERE are always, in that lane, glow-worms at one's feet and flittermice over one's head.

Glow-worms are delightful little insects. Their caterpillars glow also, but more faintly than the fully-grown beetle, with a wan, green-blue light. I should like to have a garden-full of them, for they enthusiastically devour snails. Their light, incidentally, can be switched on and off at will, and I have been told that fireflies in the tropics use a kind of morse-code of flashes to attract their mates. The light is caused by " oxidation by molecular oxygen of luciferin produced in the luminous cells "; so the experts say. That good American poet, Mr. Ogden Nash, on the other hand observes wisely:

The firefly's flame
Is something for which science has no name.
I can think of nothing eerier
Than flying around with an unidentified red
glow on a person's posterior.

As FOR bats, I love those little mice of the air and the twilight;
but they are weird creatures in every respect, and somewhat mysterious. They have no relations or affinities with any other of the
beasts. Their ancientry goes back to middle Eocene times; that
is to say according to modern calculations they have been on the
earth for more than 50 million years. Then they are the only
mammals that can truly fly. (Flying foxes can only glide.) Again
some of them, but only a few tropical ones, are blood-suckers,
vampires. I doubt if they could ever suck enough blood out of
anybody's big toe to do serious harm but their bite can transmit
hydrophobia and one or two other nasty diseases. Fortunately we
possess no such monsters here in England, and our 12 species belong
to a different family, which live mainly on insects and hibernate
in the winter. Some of them are remarkable for a physiological
singularity: they pair in the autumn, yet go to sleep unfertilised;
the sperm as it were hibernating too, so that gestation does not start
until they awaken in the spring.

But the strangest thing of all about bats is their discovery of
'radar' so many million years before we cleverbreeches thought
of it. They emit so-called 'supersonic' vibrations from the larynx.
These echo back from solid objects into the ears of the bat where
they presumably are translated into patterns like the dots on a radar
screen: but *aural*, not visual patterns. So the bat can even detect,
and avoid, a piece of black cotton stretched across a dark room.
He can do this even if he is blindfolded.

If you have very sharp ears you can be aware of the 'supersonic' vibrations. They impinge upon your ear-drum to produce
an impression like that of a slate-pencil drawn rapidly across a slate.
It is said this 'sound' is no longer perceptible by people over 40

but I certainly heard it three years ago, being then 45. This summer my pipistrelles have been silent; or can it be—ah, can it?—that I already possess this first trifling infirmity of middle-age?

Pipistrelle: a pretty name for the commonest of our bats; the scientists call him *Pipistrellus pipistrellus pipistrellus* just to make sure that you don't confuse him with any of his kith and kin. At least they used to when I was a boy; I believe they've put him into another genus since then. He is the little flittermouse which you see hawking for flies over your lawn on any summer evening—and in the winter too, on very mild nights when he wakes from his light sleep.

Have you ever seen bats hibernating?—leathery wings folded as they hang upside down, looking like dead leaves on a branch or shrivelled fruits unharvested in late autumn? Stir them up, and there's a queer crackling noise as the dry stiff wings are extended. They do not sleep sound, like hedgehogs or snakes; theirs is a shallow doze from which an echoing shout will awaken them. You find them in caves, and old hollow trees, and attics,—and presumably in belfries too, though I have never done so.

In the hand they are soft and furry (apart from the parchment-like membrane of the wings) and they have quaint little puggy faces. They fill some people with horror, goodness knows why, and some women still have a hysterical fear that they will " get into their hair ". I have never been able to understand what harm they would do in that unlikely event and in any case I am quite sure that no bat has ever flown into anybody's hair; for if its ' radar ' can pick up a thread of cotton, just as our Asdics could pick up a submerged U-boat, a woman's head of hair must represent itself to the bat as something like the Tirpitz and the Bismarck and the Graf Spee and the Scharnhorst all sailing in company!

X

'FAVOURITE COLOUR?' says the silly quiz which claims to be able to psycho-analyse me if I fill in all the answers honestly; but honestly I do not know. I am thinking of blue, and it is the blue of the Tibetan poppies, *Meconopsis Baileyi*, in Windsor Great Park. There must be a quarter of an acre of them, a carpet under the trees too lovely to be trodden on. In my garden I have three cosseted plants of this poppy, each of which produces every year three or four exquisite flowers. They are shade-loving, fanciful, and fussy about soil, difficult to keep alive in bad winters. Once I had six and now I have three, and it is very fitting that the Queen should have a quarter of an acre. This delicate, pure and somehow luminous blue is surely the loveliest colour in the world.

But then think of germander speedwell; and of hedgesparrows' eggs; and of the first gentian of the spring lifting up its trumpet in an alpine meadow only fifty yards from the snow-line. Kingfisher-blue and flax-blue and bluebell-blue, which looks curiously slaty from afar off; delphinium-blue and pale hyacinths which are as near as nothing the colour of the sky, G. K. Chesterton's " Great blue cap that always fits."

All different, and all so subtly different. And I think of all the infinite gradations of green, from lime to sage, from apple to olive. And all the yellows from primrose to that fiery, eye-hurting shade of the Siberian wallflowers, a sort of bright chrome which for some reason is visible from a greater distance than any other colour and so was used for painting our Mae Wests and our practice-bombing targets in the war. . . .

How sad to be colour-blind; and yet I suppose colour-blind

people see shades as subtle as those which delight me—but their shades do not happen to match our purely arbitrary chart? For what, after all, *is* colour? It has no real existence, it is simply a sensation produced in you and me by light waves falling on the retina at the back of the eye. The light waves produce photo-chemical changes and nerve-impulses convey an impression of these changes to the brain, which translates them into terms of ' scarlet' or ' blue '.

Yes: but how do I know that what I see, when I look at that pillar-box, is what *you* see? I can, of course, match the pillar-box colour against that of a similar pillar-box and if you agree that the match is an exact one, it merely proves that light waves of a certain frequency produce the same sensation in both of us. We describe the sensation as ' red '. But we cannot analyse it or put it in a test tube. It exists only in our minds: an idea.

So we cannot tell what the world looks like to a bird or an animal or an insect. We can deduce by various experiments that most mammals are colour-blind, not in the sense we use when speaking of humans but truly colour-blind—unable to differentiate between colours at all and seeing the world in monotone, as for instance in shades of sepia or grey. And by similar experiments we can demonstrate that bees, birds or moths can ' see ' into the ultra-violet or the infra-red, responding to the impact of light waves which produce no colour-sensation in us. For all we can tell these creatures may be aware of ranges of colour unknown to us and unknowable. For to them, too, colour is simply an idea.

And so, I suppose, was the *Meconopsis*-blue that made me catch my breath with wonder and delight as I stood in Windsor Great Park: an idea born in my brain at the prompting of nerves agitated by chemical changes occurring in a mass of minute cones in the *fovea centralis* of my retina. . . . So, at any rate, the scientists say. But the poets speak in different terms, they ransack the dictionaries for an apt word to tell us what sensation they experience when they gaze at such a flower; whether they have ever found a phrase lovely enough to match the *Meconopsis* I cannot tell, but I have never heard it.

XI

Now when the grass in the village churchyard stands as high as the tombstones, and the moon-daisies are out in it, and ' they troublesome 'ettles' (for we always drop the N) are rank along the wall—now the old man who looks after the churchyard whets his scythe and lays the tall grass in swathes with a swish-swish that's all the softer because he's got such a good edge on his blade.

In the pub in the evening he'll say to us, as he does every year:
" I bin havin' a day among the Quiet Folks."

I like the phrase; it's a friendly way of speaking of the dead. The Quiet Folks; no idle chatter there. We are not dismayed by churchyards in my part of the world; not even at night, not even at Hallowe'en! The ghosts that squeak and gibber belong to more outlandish places; at the heart of England our folks lie at ease, and as I go among the grey stones there comes into my mind the Epitaph which Aristophanes wrote on Sophocles; it is in his play *The Frogs*, and literally it goes " But he was easy there, is easy here " or, more freely:

CONTENTED AMONG THE LIVING,
CONTENTED AMONG THE DEAD.

I LIKE pottering about in country churchyards and trying to read upon old tombstones the inscriptions blurred by time, weather and moss. There is much social history to be learned there. How long some of them lived!—" Here lies Robert Pope who after a long life of industrious toil went easy to his rest in his ninety-seventh year, R.I.P." Was that word really 'easy'? I read it so, upon the crumbling stone: and if it was 'easy' it was the right word, the poet's word, lifting the epitaph out of its dull formality; but I cannot be sure.

And how briefly they lived sometimes! "Here lieth Jane Bray who dyed of the Smallpox at her Aunt Catchmay's in Gloucester, on Monday the one and twentieth of May 1711 in the 8th year of her age, much lamented; her extreme good qualities having engaged the affections of all who knew her; this stone commemorates also John Bray aged 15 who dyed of the Smallpox upon Christmas Day 1720 at the Royal Academy of Angiers in France ... so much esteem'd for his good sense and Fine Temper that every gentleman of the Academy (Foreigner as well as Briton) seemed to rival each other in paying just Honour to his memory; and the Beautys of his Person were equal to those of his Mind."

DRIVING the other day through the Berkeley Vale below Gloucester I remembered that epitaph. I also remembered two ordinary Gloucestershire names: those of James Phipps and Sarah Nelmes. I thought how surprised those humble people would have been, he a little country lad, she a dairymaid, if they could have known 150 years ago that a man passing through their village in 1955 would bear their names in mind. I dare say a good many poets, politicians, painters and prelates who were famous in the 1790's are forgotten now! But a sort of immortality was conferred upon these two, on the 14th day of May, 1790, when their village doctor took a needle and pricked a small pustule on Sarah's hand. Like many dairymaids of her time she was suffering from cowpox; and when the doctor proceeded to scratch James' arm he introduced some of her cowpox-lymph into the wound. Some six weeks later, with a courage that has rarely been matched in war, he inoculated James a second time—but with lymph taken from a victim of the smallpox. James, who was eight years old, probably had a sore arm for a week or so and wished Dr. Jenner was not so free with his needle. But he did not develop smallpox, and that is why you find his name, under the section headed VARIOLA, in all the reference books to-day.

How many millions of lives were saved by that experiment is beyond conjecture. The Parish Registers of the 18th Century, in which you can read of the burial of whole large families, all dead of the smallpox within a few weeks, give you an idea of how many it killed; a smallpox epidemic, commonplace then, makes newspaper headlines to-day. Yet there are still anti-vaccinationists; and

paradoxically they seem to be more numerous in Jenner's own county of Gloucestershire than anywhere else. Hence whenever a minor outbreak occurs there a number of people die, martyrs to their particular sort of unreason. One would be inclined to say that this was their own affair if some of the casualties were not the innocent children of know-all parents who think themselves better at weighing up scientific evidence than trained scientists!

The country doctor who performed the ' curious investigation ' (as his fellow-physicians described it at the time) was quite a remarkable fellow in other respects as well. He was interested in the migration and behaviour of birds; and his observations on the cuckoo, communicated to the Royal Society in 1788, were so original that nobody believed them—until the film camera proved him right about 1930! Earthworms fascinated him too, and his study of their habits anticipated Darwin's famous work by a century. Furthermore, this pottering, inquisitive, imaginative doctor wrote poetry; and stranger still, some of it was good poetry. He was also a pleasantly simple chap. When fame came to him—and with it a grant of £30,000 voted him by Parliament—it was suggested that he might be honoured with a Fellowship of the Royal College of Physicians. That august body, however, made the condition that he should first undergo the customary examination in the Classics. "That," said Jenner, "would be irksome beyond measure! That would be a bauble indeed! I would not do it for a diadem!" So he died without the magic letters F.R.C.P. after his name; and I don't suppose he minded.

Partly because he belongs to my own county, partly because he happens to be an ancestor of my wife, I am very interested in this poetic physician with the wide-questing mind. In particular I should like to know *how* confident he was, how certain, when he performed that astonishing experiment, the second inoculation, on the 1st of July. (If he had killed James Phipps he could easily have been charged with manslaughter!) I can't help wondering if he felt any apprehension at all, when he examined young James on, I suppose, about July 8th.

"Good morning, my boy. Er—feeling quite well?"

"Yes, thank you, doctor."

"No—er—headache? Or backache?"

"No thank you, doctor," says James, puzzled by this unwonted solicitude.

"No sickness or shivering?"

The child shakes his head and runs off to play. And Dr. Jenner, whose discovery is going to save all those millions of lives, trots off on his country round, to Mrs. Jones's confinement and Mrs.

Smith's houseful of measles, through the flat, rich country beside the Severn; and as he jogs along he is composing—who knows—a new Pastoral Poem? Or the opening sentence of a learned paper to be called, with professional modesty:

" *An Inquiry into the Causes and Effects of the Variolæ Vaccinæ.*"

Part Four

HARVEST HOME

I

WHEN most of us speak of harvest we still think of the sheaves, 'barbarous in beauty' as Gerard Manley Hopkins said; though of course the fields of golden stooks are fewer each year as the combines become more numerous. But in truth there is not one harvest but many; and at Brensham where the Cotswold farmland dips down into the fruit-growing and market-gardening country of the Evesham vale there is a whole succession of harvests from Whitsun to Elmbury Mop. First the salads and the green gooseberries; and the asparagus, which is cut from the end of April until June 26th. Thereafter, as if there were a close season for asparagus, the feathery green fern is allowed to grow unhindered and, most pleasingly, is called the 'bower'. It must not be laid low until it is tawny, a splendid lion-colour that makes the brightest patch in all the market-gardening scene. By then the strawberries, raspberries, cherries and peas have been gathered, and we are well on with the plums and the runner-beans; and by the time the first of the apples are ready you may be sure that somebody who planted them early will be picking his sprouts.

SPROUTS are our chief market-garden crop; for many of the growers they provide the bread-and-butter, fruit in a lucky season puts on the jam. They are hateful to harvest on a cold morning when the frost hangs on the tight little buds, and they are worse still to plant on a hot day in June. Take a glance at that ten-acre patch—which is not a very large one for the open countryside up at

Chipping Campden. It contains about 50,000 plants,—actually 4,840 to the acre—every one of them dibbed in by hand. There's backache for you. Alfie Perks whose market garden is at Brensham and who puts out a mere 30,000 plants each season has a recurrent nightmare about the first of June. In this appalling dream he sees, stretching before him, his seven-acre field, tilled but unplanted, which he must fill with sprouts before dusk! A good man, as a matter of fact, can dibble in about 4,000 sprout-plants a day. My friend Alfie, who seems to suffer unduly from nightmares, has a different one in the plum-picking time, when he spends about 14 hours a day up a ladder. When he goes to bed he dreams that he is clutching an enormous Victoria plum which refuses to come off the branch, tug it as hard as he will; and when he wakes up he discovers that he is pulling hard at the pear-shaped light-switch above his bed.

THE ECONOMICS behind all this backache are complex and mysterious. Every season hundreds of acres of radishes, lettuces and such-like 'catch-crops' are scrapped because they have missed the early market and it is unprofitable to harvest them; tons of cauliflowers and broccoli are fed to the pigs; pickers are even employed at good wages to pull off the pods of the runner-beans and let them rot on the ground, on the chance that more beans will form in time for a possible improvement in the price.[1] Meanwhile *on each acre* the cost of labour, rent, seeds, fertiliser and wear and tear of machinery amounts to about £150. Yet the market-gardener rarely goes bankrupt; for he farms on a system comparable with that by which a bookmaker runs his business. He 'lays off' his bets. Every crop is a gamble; and on a ten-acre holding he probably has about eight gambles a year. The odds are long, and when a bet comes off it makes up for many failures. Two acres of spring onions, harvested in an open February, may have cost the grower £350; if the unpredictable public wants them they may fetch

---

[1] If you leave the beans on the plant, and allow them to ripen, the plant naturally decides that its all-important reproductive job is over, and puts forth no more beans.

£2,000. This will pay for the unwanted radishes, the early beans killed by frost, and much else beside.

TIDY-MINDED people are shocked by the waste, in seed, artificials, labour and land; they would like to match acreage to appetite and arrange for the gardeners to provide exactly the quantity of sprouts, lettuces, parsnips or plums which the consumer is willing to consume. But this is nonsense, and it involves one of the huge fallacies of totalitarianism, that you can legislate for individual taste. Y wants his radishes early, Z wants his lettuces when he goes on holiday-picnics, A never buys anything unless it's scarce, when he thinks it's specially desirable, B never buys anything except when it's cheap. C grows tired of peas after the first helping, D perversely buys tinned carrots just when the young carrots are coming in. There is also an X in the equation. X=Nature. She represents frosts, floods, droughts, blights, unpredictable gluts and scarcities. She takes extraordinarily little notice of anybody's five-year plan.

II

Fruiting begins with the Early Prolific plums, for there are only a few scattered cherry-orchards in the Evesham vale; they belong to the Teme valley and the countryside of the Shropshire Lad. The Prolifics are like glorified sloes, hard as bullets, and are generally picked before they are ripe to satisfy a supposed passion of the townsman for plums on Bank Holiday. They only succeed in putting him off plums altogether for several weeks, wherefore our sweet and juicy Victorias are sometimes left to rot on the trees. Subsequently the townsman seems to forget his experience with the Prolifics and demands plums again. Since it is now at the end of the season we can only provide him with the late plums, huge tasteless Monarchs and sour stony plums called Birbanks. We never eat such things ourselves.

Greengages are a chancy crop—the trees bear about once in three years, and the fruits are apt to split before they are ripe if they get a summer shower on them followed by a hot sun. There are blue gages which are more delicious than any plum, and there is also, better still, a gage called a Warwickshire Drooper and best of all a very rare one called Jefferson's Drop. But these are shy bearers, and grow mostly in great walled gardens where they are cosseted by none less than the head gardeners of peers of the realm.

The pears follow the plums—those noble *Comices* and the Williams of which it is said "You must get up in the middle of the night to eat them"—because they are ripe for so short a time before they are rotten. Later come the Conference pears, and the bottling sorts, the greenery-yallery Pitmastons which taste like mangel-wurzels when they are raw. The W.I. delights in them, because they can be canned. This is the season, in every village, when even the most feckless housewife feels a provident urge to can or bottle everything she can lay her hands on. For this we must thank the W.I., which hires out canning machines, demonstrates bottling, gives prizes for the best bottles, and hires lecturers to explain the dangers of botulism. Indeed for the whole of this harvest-time the Women's Institute is so busy with its squirrel-like preparations for the hungry winter that it refrains altogether from passing its usual resolutions about the local sewage farm, rural housing, juvenile delinquency and foreign affairs.

THE DEVIL entered into me one day in the guise of the Muse of Mr. Ogden Nash, to whose poetry I am devoted, and I wrote some lines about the W.I. This is how they begin:

Since Mr. Ogden Nash has lent me his Muse and his Manner
I propose to make a song in praise of the canner
Of plums and tomatoes, the churner of butter, the baker of cakes
(Which is done in the intervals between singing that poem of Blake's).
The confector of jam and the bottler of fruit—
In short (take a deep breath now) the WOMEN'S INSTITUTE.

At this stage I began to have some misgivings, for though it is permissible to make jokes about the Mother of Parliaments now and then, we have to think twice before we speak lightly of the W.I., because—

Like all good English institutions it is a little bit solemn,
And if she reads this column
It is quite probable that Mrs. Hamilton-Treasure will say to her committee,
" It was well-meant I daresay, but I think it was a pity."
And Mrs. King the treasurer who is always winning prizes with her honey
Will add " If you ask me I don't think it is funny."

Come Rain, Come Shine

Nevertheless I shall finish my poem,
If only to show 'em
That a mere man realises the importance of all their doings,
Which range from the making of rag-rugs to all manner of bakings and
*   boilings and stewings.*

Bless them, they even had a talk on poetry, sandwiched in the middle
Of a performance on the fiddle;
And a demonstration of the use of Nasturtium Seeds as a substitute for
*   Capers;*
But one of our local papers
Got the thing wrong of course and had to print an apology:
" The Talk to the W.I. on Thursday by Lady Blank was entitled
*   ' A Floral Anthology ',*
Being on the subject of poetry and not on the Manurial Value of Compost
*   in the Flower Garden*
As stated in our previous issue.   We beg her Ladyship's pardon."

But poetry is nothing to Them, they take it in their stride.
Just look at the current programme for Michaelmastide:
" Fowl-Plucking Competition Open to All
(N.B.: The fowls must be alive when brought to the Village Hall) ";
" Lantern Lecture on the Cathedrals of France ";
" Evening of Round Games followed by a Dance—
Husbands may be Brought ".
" Mozart Recital by Miss Tiddley-Push, followed by a short
Open Discussion on Bacon-curing and the Making of Home-made Wine
(Please bring recipe books). *On Thursday, if fine,*
Visit to Lady Blank's Garden; if unsuitable weather,
Hat-trimming Competition with bits and pieces, flowers, fur and feather.
Afterwards a Brains Trust, the Chairman will be Mrs. Pidgeon
(No questions, if you please, on politics or religion)."

My goodness, it makes you think
When you pass that terrifying notice-board on your way to have a drink,

Harvest Home

And to idle away your time talking about horses
While They, perhaps, are listening to a lecture on Sauces!
It gives you the willies
To think of all the chutneys and piccalillies
They are making for your benefit *while you sozzle your beer;*
So bless 'em, the little busybees, say I; let's give 'em a cheer!

III

THE APPLES provide the last of the harvests off the trees. The first of them is Beauty of Bath and the last are those old-fashioned russets which hang on to the trees long after the last yellow leaves have fallen. In between come the pippins and the Laxtons and the Bramleys, and the Blenheims which by tradition we always pick on October Fair Day, when the Colonel, you will remember, by tradition always caught his first pike.

But there are also the nameless, innumerable, cider apples and hard perry pears, which grow upon old beautiful trees which only a born Reformer could bring himself to cut down. They were planted in the days when every farm made its own cider, and drank its own cider, several hundred gallons of it, during the hot days between the beginning of haysel and the end of the corn-harvest. Nowadays harvesting is less thirsty work, and most of the cider-mills have fallen into disuse. We are not really cider-drinkers at Brensham; though we took to it during the war when beer was short, with some remarkable consequences, since farm cider is about three times as alcoholic as beer. Some of it contained bellyaches, thick heads and fighting devils; so we gladly returned to our beer, and the heaps of red apples rot beneath the trees. Perhaps we could make use of them if we turned our surplus cider into apple-jack, as the Canadians do, or Calvados, as they call the distilled spirit in Normandy. It is a powerful drink that warms the cockles. I found two bottles of it during the invasion, in the Bar Normandie at Arromanches, and invited three indestructible civilians (who had emerged from the ruins as civilians do when the battle passes them by) to share them with me and so celebrate the

Liberation. The celebration started rather badly for as I opened the first bottle there was an appalling bang, a naval shell landed a little way down the street, and one of the civilians, looking out of the window, informed me gloomily " You have just liberated the café of Madame Lebrun." However, I was still feeling somewhat excited at having set foot once more on the sacred soil of France, so I lifted my glass with enthusiasm and cried:

" *A la victoire!* "

Whereupon three stolid russet-faced Norman peasants raised their glasses too, but only a little, and without looking up growled sombrely:

" *A la paix.*"

WE COULD make apple-jack, I believe, as the North Americans do, by freezing the cider instead of distilling it. They put it out in shallow milk-pans during hard frosts, break off the ice each night, and ultimately find themselves in possession of a residual liquid which is so alcoholic that it will no longer freeze: and that ought to be strong enough for anybody. It has occurred to me that we could carry out the same process in a refrigerator; but perhaps the Customs and Excise would then maintain that our frig. was an illicit still? At any rate we have not tried the experiment; and the cider apples remain unharvested, clinging late to their shapely trees, scarlet enough to tempt Eve herself but, like that Apple, so bitter in the after-taste!

BUT was it an apple? I was taken to task about this by a friend of mine who is a Scot and therefore has theological disputation bred in his very bones. " Who told you," he demanded severely " that the Forbidden Fruit which you likened to a Worcester Pearmain on page 98 of your last book was an apple at all? Go back to the Book of Genesis and hang your head in shame."

And of course he is right; anyhow I don't propose to take him on in argument, for his ancestors were the sort of men who would debate for a fortnight on end about how many angels could dance on the point of a needle. I re-read Genesis and true enough the only positive thing which it tells us about the Tree of Knowledge is that it was 'good for food' and 'pleasant to the eye' and 'a tree to be desired to make one wise'. Why, then, have I and incidentally half the poets of Christendom assumed it to have been an apple? "Eve, with the apple half way to her lips," wrote Ralph Hodgson. "And for an apple damn'd mankind," wrote Thomas Otway. But what does John Milton say in *Paradise Lost*? You have to wade through nearly 9,000 lines to find it; and then the Serpent's account of the Tree runs as follows:

> *A goodly Tree far distant to behold*
> *Loaden with fruit of fairest colours mixt,*
> *Ruddy and gold: I nearer drew to gaze;*
> *When from the boughs a savoury odour blow',*
> *Grateful to appetite, more pleas'd my sense*
> *Than smell of sweetest fennel. . . .*

which is odd, because fennel as we know it has a perfectly beastly smell.

"So talked the spirited sly snake"—in Milton's delightful phrase. He led Eve through thickets and swamps to the Forbidden Tree, and they both indulged in a great deal of metaphysical argument before

> *An eager appetite, raised by the smell*
> *So savoury of that fruit. . . .*
> *Solicited her longing eye;*

Still no mention, you see, of an apple. Searching such other authorities as I can think of, in the hope of confounding my Scottish friend, I discover that " the Mahometan doctors aver the Forbidden Fruit to have been the Indian fig, because fig-leaves were employed to cover the disobedient pair when they felt shame."

But I don't think a fig would tempt anybody. A mango might, for it looks very luscious and handsome as it hangs upon the branch, though when you begin to eat it you suffer a sharp disillusion, for it tastes like turpentine. A tangerine? It has a sweet smell as described by Milton, and it is pleasant to the eye, and tempting to the thirsty. But how about a nectarine, an apricot or a peach? That would fit Milton's description that it was " ruddy and gold." I'll put my money on the peach; for indeed every time I pluck a peach from the little tree which I planted against a south wall in my garden I am aware, now I come to think of it, of a kind of awe, a sense of " Did I really grow this delicious thing myself? " You never feel like that with apples or pears or plums; but the young peach-tree bears only a dozen or so fruits each season, and it is something of an occasion, almost a ceremony, to pick one of them. The hour must be just right, the fruit sun-warmed, the wall behind it hot to the touch, yet if you were to delay but a little longer the wasps or the birds would have forestalled you. A peach eaten at such a time is surely the most exquisite fruit of all, and I am prepared to believe that such a fruit may have hung tantalisingly, just within reach, upon the Tree of the Knowledge of Good and Evil. I am almost prepared to believe that the tree was an ancestor of the kind of peach called *Alexandre Noblesse*, which I have planted against the wall in my garden, where each September it holds forth its ancient temptation to various daughters of Eve.

IV

Now the bulb-catalogues come along, which as I told you always have such a deplorable effect upon my finances; and this year to complete my ruin there was a catalogue of shrubs which persuaded me that it would be a long-term economy to plant with little trees a part of the garden which in theory is occupied by herbaceous flowers, in practice mainly by weeds. This catalogue, though it was sent to me free, proved better reading than a good many books which cost half a guinea; but it tempted me to spend a fiver on the shrubs. They duly arrived most cunningly wrapped in twisted straw, each with its name on a label tied round its stem; all I had to do was to dig the holes, decide which was to go where, and then, leaning on the spade, imagine what they would look like when I was half a dozen years older.

My choice from the catalogue was made easier because I am full of prejudices about shrubs. I hate pale pink flowers, which rules out the various Prunuses and Almonds which, the booklet ecstatically told me, " would produce blossoms as delicately tinted as a maiden's blush." I also hate conifers in a garden, at any rate in an English garden, though I shall never forget the cypresses in the gardens of the Generalife at Granada in Spain, small neat dark trees of an exquisite gravity, growing around little lawns in the middle of which fountains played, and one orange-tree, laden with fruits, stood beside each fountain. The bright oranges set off the almost-black cypresses, and there was a scent of tobacco-flower on the heavy air, and I could imagine how, in the days when Moorish princes lived in the Alhambra, the veiled ladies of the harem would walk at evening among those trim straight trees and trip on tiny feet across the cool green lawns to pluck a juicy tangerine. However, I can't grow oranges, so I didn't buy a cypress. I did, however, treat myself to one exotic tree, a Gum Cistus, which has evergreen leaves and in late summer puts forth huge pale yellow flowers with chocolate centres. And I bought a Strawberry Tree, which is supposed to produce weird pendant fruits like strawberries; they are not, however, edible except by the birds.

I bought a flowering currant for the sake of its red lambikins-tails in the spring, and a Japanese maple for the sake of its scarlet leaves in the autumn, a Buddleia for its butterflies, and two sallows because of their golden ' palms ' which attract the bees by day and the moths by night whenever March is mild. I hope, at any rate, that they will produce the authentic pussy-willows, which turn from silver-grey to gold; but these, I have just recollected, come out on the male shrubs only. Male and female created He the sallow; and the female flowers are dingy and green. Plants which have flowers of different sexes are often a puzzle to gardeners; a dear old lady asked me what to do about her melons, explaining in an embarrassed whisper: " I think, dear, that they've all turned out to be *men*."

A Choisya for its heavy-scented white flowers, a Philadelphus which most people wrongly call orange-blossom and a Syringa, which most people think is the Latin name of Orange-blossom, but is really our old-fashioned lilac. . . . A Berberis to burn like the embers of a fire in the very early spring, a Daphne, a Forsythia which some spring will cover itself with blossom exactly the colour of scrambled eggs, a Fuchsia, a Broom such as Plantagenet kings wore in their helmets; a Silver Birch and a Wych Elm, a Laburnum to shower down its golden rain; a Lemon Verbena, so that I may crush its scented leaves beneath my fingers; a Myrtle; and for its name a Rose of Sharon, though I have never seen it in flower and already I begin to suspect that it is not very different from any other St. John's Wort. That completes my list, save for a little Magnolia, of which my catalogue proudly boasts " It will produce globular white flowers 8–10 inches across intermittently throughout the summer; *height* 30 to 40 feet; *spread* 25 to 35 feet."

But it grows, warns the catalogue, very slowly and at the present moment it is four feet tall. So as the old fellow who helped me dig the holes said to me a trifle grimly as we firmed down the soil around it: "Us'll not be gettin' toothache when *her* puts forth her flowers."

V

I LOVE the slow languishing days between summer and autumn, which are often the stillest of the year. I love walking along woodsides so silent that you can hear the first leaves fall. A pigeon suddenly startled crashes through the branches overhead and makes me jump; its headlong plunge tears a feather or two from its breast and the feathers seem to hang in the very sky, I can count ten slowly before they fall to earth.

Especially in this weather I enjoy walking before breakfast in a morning mist which makes the most ordinary things look strange and turns the familiar landscape into one of fantasy. A cockerel, crowing on somebody's wall, looks like a heraldic bird, crested, ominous, prophesying doom. Our little hill, only 900 feet high, is Kangchenjunga at least; old sheep, furred with moisture so that they look almost silver, appear and vanish. Ibex! The church bell ringing for Mass in the valley below is the bell of some monastery calling the lamas to worship!

These are mushroomy mornings; and along the edge of a wood on Brensham Hill there are fields where if I get up *very* early, earlier than the old woman who lives in the cottage in the wood, I can see the mushrooms as big as dinner-plates, their moist tops shining in the first light of the dawn. But always about six the old woman comes forth with her basket; and thereafter no mushrooms are to be seen.

MY WAY back from the hill takes me through the village, and I learn some quaint sociological facts. For example, the first thing the average country cottager does when he gets up leisurely at

about 7 a.m. on a Sunday morning is to appear in his doorway with a teapot in his hand and to tip yesterday's tea-leaves out of the pot before he makes a cup for himself and the missus. But people have curiously different ideas about tea-leaves. One man sprinkles them on his garden path with an expression of malice as if he thought he was destroying the weeds; another puts them lovingly round his sprout-plants in the hope that they will act as a fertiliser. A third shakes them into his pig-trough, holding the view that they will give his pig a sleek coat; a fourth jauntily chucks them over the fence into the neighbour's garden.

THE THING that really astonishes me, whenever I walk in the early morning, is the prevalence of cats. I would never have believed that the cat-population was so large. I meet them hunting at lane-side and in the woodland ride, stealthy, slinking and feral, quite different from the *alter ego* which by day purrs upon the hearth or sits so smugly in the old lady's lap. And I meet them walking home: ginger, tabby, black, Persian, tortoiseshell, fitcher, renegade Siamese; long-haired, short-haired, sleek, scruffy, some with draggle-tails and some with tails curled triumphantly like umbrella-handles.

I greet them all politely, for cats like to receive a courteous address, and they look at me with all kinds of feline and human expressions, among which the only one which is absent is a sense of shame.

James Fisher told me that some successor of Darwin associated a preponderance of cats with a preponderance of old maids. He was improving on Darwin's ingenious example of a chain of relationships in Nature. Darwin propounded that

> *Cats destroy mice;*
> *Mice destroy the nests of humble bees;*
> *Humble bees pollenate the wild clover;*
> Ergo *fewer cats = more mice = fewer*
> *humble bees = less clover because*
> *humble bees are the only insects which*
> *can insert their tongues into the*
> *clover-flowers.*

I think this is not quite true, because at its second blossoming the wild clover produces shorter flowers; but it's a beautiful instance of how ecology works. If you accept that there is a natural association between old maids and cats you can relate the number of old maids to the abundance or scarcity of clover.

But in fact in our village almost everybody keeps cats. An estimate of the total cat population of this island is 14 million, one to every four humans (E. M. Nicholson, *Birds and Men*). —That is at least one to every household. How surprising that this jungly creature, as it originally was, should have achieved, of all the mammals, the closest association with man! I don't know when we first ' kept '—for we have never ' tamed '—the little creatures; the ancient Egyptians certainly treated them with honour,—which makes it all the stranger that in the whole of the Bible there is not a single mention of a cat! This is surely an omission as mysterious as Shakespeare's of the Avon, which word does not appear anywhere in the canon of his works.

THE-OLD-WOMAN-WHO-LIVES-IN-THE-WOOD, she who forestalls me

over the mushrooms, was already old, or seemed so, when I was a little boy. She practised then the trade of a Wisewoman; and we children, birdsnesting, butterfly-hunting, would peer in awe over the gate at her little garden full of herbs, pennyroyal and rosemary and bergamot with its scarlet tags. Sometimes she asked us in, and gave us cooling drinks of lime-tip tea, which she said cured everything and would also make us grow. " Drink enough of it," she said, " and you'll be taller than the trees! " This frightened us: we saw ourselves growing like Jack's beanstalk, we saw ourselves long and thin and sinister as the scissors-man who cut off Struwwelpeter's fingers, no, no, we wouldn't have any more lime-tip tea thank you, we didn't want to be taller than the trees!

There were herbs of all kinds drying on the Wisewoman's sun-drenched wall, and the parlour was full of a sweet smell of pot-pourri. I suppose she would have been called a White Witch, 200 years ago: a somewhat dangerous profession, because if things went wrong your customers were apt to change their minds suddenly and decide that you were a Black one! But this old woman was well thought of, even by my doctor-uncles, whose patients sometimes visited her in secret; she made a modest living, enough anyhow for her simple needs, for there are always a few people to whom Magic makes a stronger appeal than Reason. Indeed we all play with Magic now and then; we turn our money, revolve till we are giddy, and bow to the new moon; we try hard not to see the tails of piebald ponies; we refrain from walking under ladders lest it bring us bad luck in the future, even at the risk of the immediate bad luck of being run over by a bus when we step off the pavement. Few of us are rational in all things at all seasons; which is lucky for the pedlars of cure-alls, who even in this scientific age are enabled to keep the wolf from the door.

But they used to do better than that. Don Lopus, the Illustrious Spanish Doctor, who travelled the country with a zany during the 17th century, made a fortune out of his quackery, and probably deserved to, for his sheer eloquence:

" Here is a Powder concealed in a paper. I will only tell you, it is the Powder that made Venus a goddess (given her by Apollo), that kept her perpetually young, cleared her wrinkles, firmed her gums, fill'd her skin, colour'd her hair, from her derived to Helen and the Sack of Troy! Unfortunately lost till now, in this our age it was happily recovered by a studious antiquary out of some Ruins of Asia, who sent a moiety of it to the Court of France; the rest (at this present) remains with me, extracted to a Quintessence, so that wherever it but touches in youth it perpetually preserves, in age restores the complexion, seats your teeth till they dance like virginal jacks, firm as a wall, and makes them white as ivory that were black as hell."

Dr. Edith Sitwell in her *English Eccentrics* has made a fine collection of these half-crazy quacks, who not only sold new remedies for old diseases but invented plenty of new diseases as well. *The Rare and Wonderful Doctress*, in a book published about 1690, offered to cure " the Glimm'ning of the Gizzard, the Quavering of the Kidneys, the Wambling Trot "; another benefactor of the human race had remedies for " the greatest Causes of the most common Distempers Incident to the Body of Man, the Names of which are as follows: The Strong Fives, the Marthambles, the Moon-Pall, the Hockogrockle." . . .

The old-woman-who-lived-in-the-wood made no such extravagant claims as that; but she certainly cured warts, which was more than my doctor-uncles could do, though they possessed frozen carbon dioxide with which to burn them away. The warts almost always came back; but when the old woman anointed them with spittle, hey-presto, they vanished for good!

VI

O<small>N THESE</small> mushroomy mornings when there has been a heavy dew every furze-bush on the hill, every bracken-frond, is silvered with cobwebs. I don't suppose the spiders are specially industrious at this time of year; the cobwebs are always there on a summer morning, but the dewdrops make them visible from a long way off. (I have seen a whole field, in the dawn, looking as if it was covered with a sheet of glass.)

It is somewhat awe-inspiring to reflect that each one of those multitudinous webs is woven with five or six different kinds of silk spun out of 600 little taps each connected by a separate tube to a separate gland in the spider's body; in those of some species no less than 13,000 individual lines are used to join the spokes together. They are masterpieces of complexity and as beautiful as anything we can spin out of nylon, but their purpose, of course, is simply to trap and to kill. A spider's web is surely the cleverest, wickedest trap ever devised by any of the occupants of the earth; which is not altogether surprising, since the spiders have had some 300 million years in which to perfect it.

Their method of killing their prey (which they rope, like a bullock, or swathe in bandages like a mummy, before they drag it to the slaughter) is a model of efficient calculated butchery. Ruthless efficiency marks the whole life-history of these always horrifying, often beautiful and (in terms of evolution) infinitely wise creatures. The feminist society in which they live is pitilessly efficient. It is, of course, by no means unusual in nature to find that the male is a minor functionary, mass-produced and prodigally cast away as soon as his brief but essential task has been performed, but some species of spiders have gone much farther than that. The male is not quite finished with when mating is done; he has one more function to perform; and that is to provide a juicy and substantial meal for his lady. She hugs him so tight that it is difficult for the observer to see where love ends and hunger begins; but that crucial moment comes at last and soon he lies quiet within her arms and she is contentedly sucking his blood. Who knows but that in her little consciousness she believes she loves him still? But alas, by morning he is no more than a dry husk, shrivelled, dessicated, soon to be blown away on the winds.

In contrast to her utilitarian and contemptuous attitude to her husband the female spider displays a heroic and rather touching devotion to her eggs. Some species build an intricate cocoon for them as big as a pigeon's egg and in doing so use up the last of their silk. Nature provides them with no more, so lacking rope to snare her prisoners and to bind them when snared, the female spider starves to death. Mr. John Crompton, to whose book on *The Spider* I am indebted for these fascinating facts, describes her last hours as follows:

" Having made that super nursery, insulated, waterproof and furnished with the richest silks, satins, teazled floss and blankets, the mother takes no more interest in her eggs or young. . . . She will never hear the stirring of tiny bodies in the sacred inner creche. Nor would she be interested if she did. As far as she is concerned the end is come. That once portly matron is a withered hag and soon dies."

But other species carry their eggs about in a sort of wallet, like a large pill, strapped to their undersides; and when the little ones hatch they let them ride on their backs for a further six months or so—200 young ones riding on their mother as if she were an elephant at the zoo. The indefatigable Fabre tried to find out how many children she could carry; and the experiment was a simple one because when female spiders meet they generally fight to the death. Fabre therefore introduced three females into a jar and watched the subsequent dog-fight.

Their respective offspring watched also, with some alarm, having dismounted and hidden in a corner. The victorious virago, when she had slain her two opponents, allowed all 600 babies to climb on to her back, and presumably bore them about until they were ready to fly.

Yes, fly! Nature distributes her spiders about the world as she scatters dandelion seed, by parachute. The parachute is a tiny silken thread; and upon a day when there is no wind, but a steady upward current from the warm ground, the aeronauts are snatched up into the sky, where they may sail up to as high as 14,000 feet and travel hundreds of miles—even, perhaps, from continent to continent across the oceans!

THESE little animals have ballooned through the skies, crawled upon the earth, or dwelt in underwater diving-bells during a period 300 times longer than man's existence. They have endured vast climatic changes and have colonised every part of the globe except its extremities. To compare our evolutionary experience with theirs would be as if to compare an infant of three with the late George Bernard Shaw at the height of his powers. Since we do not seriously compete with them for food or environment, there is no conflict between us; indeed they are our allies against the flies, and the co-inhabitants of our dwellings. But whether we or the spiders represent the more 'successful' experiment, from Nature's point of view, seems to me a bit doubtful; on our different planes of existence, perhaps we both have an equal right to call ourselves the lords of creation. Certainly the water-spiders make a better diving-bell than we do; the aeronaut-spiders take the air with less danger, and much less fuss; the web-spinners without any machinery save their own most wonderful little bodies make our fully-fashioned hose look like the clumsy knitting of a child!

VII

ALL THREE of our native woodpeckers pay a visit occasionally to my three acres of orchard and garden: the Great Green, which countrymen call the Yaffle because of its laughing cry or the Stock Eagle because of the way it perches on the trunks of trees; the Greater Spotted, black-and-white and crimson; and the Lesser Spotted with a red crest and rich buff throat, a gaudy and tropical-looking little bird. The Greater Spotted is my favourite: he loves almonds, and we happen to have a very fruitful almond-tree so he visits us during the autumn to gather his own nut-harvest. We don't trouble to collect the almonds when they fall, for their shells are as hard as concrete and it is a tedious business to break them up one by one with a hammer to get at the kernels inside. The Greater Spotted, however, possesses a beak that is more efficient than a hammer; he picks up the almonds, one at a time, and carries each to a neighbouring pear tree where he has made, or found for himself, a small convenient hole. He uses this hole as if it were a vice, jamming the almond in it tightly, hammering away until the shell cracks, and cleverly extracting the kernel. Last spring I swept up half a sack of broken almond-shells from under the pear-tree; and I reckoned I'd bought his company cheap for the 50 lbs. or so of nuts which they represented.

The Great Green spends most of his time on the lawn, eating ants; it plunges its bill into their little hillocks and picks the ants up with its tongue. It has a real passion for them, and when it has found a plentiful store it becomes so absorbed in ant-eating that it even ignores the cats, who stalk it in play but never pounce, regarding it with suspicion as a bird outside their ken.

It is welcome to my ants, which swarm on the lawn and make it uncomfortable for anybody who sits there. I am all the more wary of them since I heard a true story of Ants in the Pants concerning a young man and his newly betrothed who went from London to Brighton on a day excursion and spent the afternoon in pleasant dalliance among some sandhills near the town. In the train on the way back to London the young man became aware of an acute itching: he had been sitting on an antheap. So he hastened to the toilet and, removing his trousers, shook them vigorously out of the window. At that moment an express passed by in the opposite direction; the wind of its speed plucked the trousers from his grasp and deposited them on the embankment. The young man remained trouserless in the toilet until at last his girl sought him out and he explained to her through the keyhole what was the matter. By now the train was coming into Victoria, and as soon as it drew up to the platform the girl jumped out and went in search of the station-master. It took a long time to explain *why* her young man was immolated in the toilet without his trousers, but at last the station-master understood the situation and managed to borrow a spare pair of trousers from a porter. But alas, as with the station-master she hastened along the platform to rescue her beloved the train started off on its return journey to Brighton! And in vain the station-master waved the trousers, and in vain the young man leaning out of the window pleaded for help. Back he went trouserless to Brighton, where it is to be hoped he was at last rescued from his absurd predicament.

No: I do not like ants. Their little sting is as sharp as a pin and the formic acid which they inject into the bite causes a quick and uncomfortable swelling. Formic acid is named after the ants, which belong to a family called the *Formicidae*; and if you want to demonstrate how much of it their bodies contain you can let an ant loose on a piece of blue litmus paper; as it runs about there it will leave a thin red trail behind it, where the acid has changed the colour of the litmus.

However, my Great Green Woodpecker thrives on formic acid;

and he must have a tough and horny tongue, for he sweeps up the ants upon it and takes no notice of their stings. Possibly they add a pleasant piquancy to his meal, as red pepper tickles our own appetite, or the hottest Madras curry gives delight to old Colonels.

VIII

As the autumn approaches you can hardly travel a mile along a country main road without finding the squashed remains of a hedgehog which has been run over during the previous night. The casualties among hedgehogs must be enormous, and yet there seems to be no evidence that the animal has become any less common since the advent of the motor-car. I don't know why this slaughter of the hedgehogs should be a phenomenon of late autumn, —for you find far fewer victims in the spring and summer. Can it be that the little beasts, which have sniffed the first chilly air and are looking for winter-quarters at the hedge-roots, are already slumberous and slothful with the heaviness of approaching hibernation—so that they do not move quickly enough to get out of the way of the wheels? Certainly the hedgehog can run swiftly when it wants to, despite its short legs; and being so lowly in its gait it is unlikely to be dazzled by the car lights, as rabbits are.

One sees a lot of wild animals during a night drive through country lanes. Not long ago, as I was coming over the Cotswolds, two lovely foxes crossed the road in front of my car. One of them, momentarily blinded, paused on the grass verge with its head cocked sideways, one fore paw in the air, long brush swishing. Then I chased a hare which galloped in front of the car at a good 20 m.p.h. before it jumped the stone wall in one glorious bound. Rats, weasels, and one stoat ran across the road belly to the ground like little clockwork toys. And a barnowl, looking enormous, glided into the beam and out of it like some pallid ghost of Hallowe'en. Moths too: for it was a mild night, and there are quite a few sorts which fly in November. If you look at your car's bonnet after a night-journey you can count scores of dead ones stuck on to it. I have often wondered whether this has any effect upon the total population in the case of the rarer species; but as with the hedgehogs, there is no sign of a decline in numbers which could be ascribed to this cause. I suppose that insect populations are so enormous, and the insects so proliferous that the loss of 100,000 or even 1,000,000 would make no perceptible difference.

HERE's another mystery of the autumn: what kills the shrews which one finds all over the place at this time of year, lying dead with no apparent injury? There must surely be an annual autumnal epidemic among them, possibly a virus disease; but how swift and sudden must be its effects, since apparently it overtakes them and strikes them down before they can crawl to any hole or shelter,—which is the instinctive aim of all animals about to die. Dozens of naturalists, including Gilbert White himself, have been puzzled by this mortality of the shrews, and I have never read a satisfactory explanation of it. Incidentally, why do cats always refuse to eat shrews, though they will catch them, play with them, and kill them? They must have an unpleasant taste or smell; the other day when Scarlett offered a baby shrew to one of her kittens, I watched the kitten sniff it with obvious distaste, pick it up, drop it, and finally retreat from it as if to say " *That* stinking thing! No thank you! " But owls eat them, as do most of the smaller predatory birds; indeed owls' pellets—those lumps of regurgitated fur and feathers— often contain a high proportion of the fragmentary skull-bones of shrews.

IX

SHIFTING a hundredweight sack of pig-meal, I found beneath it a nest of new-born rats, unpleasing creatures at which Candy, the senior cat, being called to dispatch them looked with horror, twitching her nose. Then she gave me one of those very superior cat-glances, slant-eyed as a Russian ballerina, with which human folly is gently reproved by felines; and shrugging her shoulders she stalked away. The little rats were naked and distasteful and pinkish; and I thought with revulsion of the mouse-babies which the Chinese are said to eat, candied in sugar. I drowned them without compunction, after trying to calculate how many great-grandchildren they might have within three years if I didn't.

IT IS fascinating to consider the effect which this little animal has had upon the course of history. In the great pandemic of the sixth century A.D. it scuttled about the Roman Empire bearing the germs of bubonic plague to such effect that it killed about half the population of that great empire and perhaps contributed to its fall. In 1348, and the half-dozen years that followed, it slew some 25 million Europeans by means of the Black Death, and in 1665 the same rat-borne bacillus, this time called the Great Plague, killed 60,000 in London alone. In collaboration with its own parasitic louse, and the invisible bug Rickettsia, which causes typhus, the rat has successfully intervened in many of our wars. When Ferdinand and Isabella were besieging Granada in 1492 it decimated the defenders, so that resistance collapsed, and Islam was expelled from Europe. But the rat is impartial in matters of faith, and Christian armies have known its deadly power. With its weapon of typhus it added to the rout of Napoleon's army in the retreat from Moscow, and it completely held up the German invasion of Serbia in the first world war. The consequences of these scuttlings to and fro are incalculable. The rat may have won more wars than the generals have lost.

WHAT an odd paradox, that the rodent thrives best in close association with its chief persecutor and sworn foe! It flourishes wherever men are; though every man's hand is against it. Few of us can resist a rat-hunt. Indeed the sudden appearance of a rat has an extraordinary effect upon otherwise sane people. The Colonel for instance became apoplectic at the sight of a rat; he danced a savage war-dance, brandishing his walking-stick. He would waste half a day sitting outside a rat-run with a .22 rifle upon his knees; if the rat came out it was promptly bowled over and provided the excuse for an extra whisky when he told the story in the Swan. For some reason, anybody who kills a rat cannot resist telling the tale in detail, as if it were big game. I took part in a broadcast with a man who was supposed to talk about country affairs in general, but who suddenly said to himself, like Boswell's Dr. Grainger (who was notable for the banality of his verse) " Come, Muse, let's sing of rats "—and proceeded to describe a rat-hunt with such verisimilitude that he knocked over the microphone.

ONLY YESTERDAY I saw from my study-window a sudden commotion in my neighbour's farmyard; there was much shouting and an explosion of running figures, so that for a moment I thought there had been an accident and that somebody's hand had been caught in the chaff-cutter. Then I saw Bill haring across the yard with a pitchfork, Bill's terrier yelping round the corner of the cowhouse, and Margie was throwing a stone with a surprisingly professional action, like a smart cover-point chucking in at the wicket. All work ceased, and the whole rout of four men, two girls and a dog disappeared into the big barn, whence came intermittent yells and hollers for the next ten minutes. At last they returned triumphant, and Bill was carrying a big rat by the tail.

AND NOW upon my desk a printed postcard tells me that " The Rodent Control Officer will call . . ."

As usual, it makes me furious. I shall be only too pleased to see the ratcatcher, who is a decent fellow; but " Rodent Control Officer "!—I dare say before long somebody will start a Rodent Control Officers' Association and appoint a Public Relations Officer to make protests in the press about music-hall jokes against Rodent Control Officers.

I shall remind my ratcatcher of

> *Hamelin's town in Brunswick*
> *By famous Hanover city*

which once suffered from a plague of rats. I shall ask him whether he thinks the Pied Piper was a past President of the Rodent Control Officers' Association.

X

CONSIDERING the things we do to rats—the murderous virus which we seek to spread among them, the phosphorus poisons which cause a raging thirst so that the rat drinks and thereby burns away its throat, œsophagus and stomach—is it not surprising that the ' humanitarians ' have made such a fuss about myxomatosis and rabbits? I suppose it's because the rat is less attractive, less romantic, than the furry, cuddly bunny of our childhood.

I lose patience with these sentimentalists, with the R.S.P.C.A. that behaved in this matter like a gaggle of soppy schoolgirls, and with the Minister of Agriculture who allowed himself to be stampeded by a lot of M.P.s who were frightened of their more hysterical constituents, and made it an offence to spread the disease artificially.

Many of the people who wrote letters to their M.P.s, or even to the press, on the subject of myxomatosis, didn't even know what it was. I read one such letter expressing the charitable wish that the man who ' invented ' myxomatosis, as well as those who ' let it loose upon God's creatures ', would die very slowly of some disease equally distressing. But of course no *man* invented myxomatosis; you might perhaps say God invented it; for it is caused by a minute living organism which has long been endemic among rabbits in South America. Thence it was introduced deliberately into Australia and perhaps accidentally into France; and from France it came, almost certainly through no agency of man, to south-eastern England. Subsequently it spread almost all over the country and its spread admittedly was assisted here and there by the deliberate act of farmers. But the scientists told us that to spread it artificially was probably, in the long run, humane; for by doing so we might have produced a great 'epizootic' or pandemic which would more or less wipe rabbits out. Otherwise it was likely that a fairly large rabbit population would continue to suffer from the disease in a series of local outbreaks for very many years. (This seems to be happening.) So if you can measure suffering quantitatively, a rapid spread of myxomatosis would have caused less suffering than a slow one.

However, let me reiterate that man did *not* invent it; and its virus has as much right to be called one of God's creatures as the rabbit has, as the stoat, snake, octopus, snail, slug, liverfluke or the germ of bubonic plague has. For it would surely be heresy to ascribe to God the creation only of what we consider to be charming or beautiful things, say song-birds, butterflies and rabbits.

Now God did not enjoin upon His creatures, apparently, that they should live together in peace. They are continually at war; and unless they were so, most of them would become extinct. The spider, the bat and the swallow would die out if they ceased to prey upon flies; the flies would die out if their grubs ceased to prey upon or parasitise various other creatures; and so on. In fact, were it not for this ceaseless interacting warfare of all creatures that on earth do dwell none of the beasts, birds, butterflies and plants with which we are familiar would have come into being; for they were all evolved as a direct consequence of the battle for survival, growing let us say long legs for fleeing or chasing, sharp teeth for tearing at the living flesh of their fellows, protective colouring to conceal them from their foes, and so on. The 'balance of nature' is simply a balance existing at any given moment between a large number of competitive, ruthless and often murderous organisms each struggling for more than their fair share of the available food, water, light and living-space. Man is himself one of the competitors.

That is to say, *you* are one of the competitors. Even if you are a vegetarian you are in this battle. Try planting a patch of cabbage or a row of lettuce, and thereafter letting 'Nature take its course'.

You will be lucky if the other vegetarians (birds, caterpillars, aphides, rabbits, wireworms and such like) leave you 10 per cent of the crop. If man tried to exist on 10 per cent of his crops he would probably become extinct in a few hundred years; or he would continue upon the earth only in the form of a few pitiful, scattered tribes. I will assume that even the humanitarians do not consider this end desirable, and are prepared (personally or by proxy) to poison, trap, shoot, or starve some of their fellow-inhabitants of the planet in order that their own species may survive.

So it boils down to this: *how* shall we kill our competitor the rabbit or our competitor the rat? We have long been accustomed to poison the rat in a number of peculiarly painful ways. We have waged war against the charming bunny by shooting, snares and gin traps for hundreds of years. Shooting sends away a percentage of rabbits to die most painfully of gangrenous wounds; around each dead, snared rabbit a circle of pounded earth testifies to its dying agonies; gin traps?—can you ever begin to imagine the terror, the pain, of being caught in a gin?

Myxomatosis is just another weapon. We do not know for sure if it is more or less cruel than, say, the gin. It seems to engender discomfort rather than pain, apathy rather than fear. Most diseases carry as it were their own anæsthetics; Nature by dulling the senses provides mercifully a limit to pain. My own observation, for what it is worth, suggests that myxomatosis, disgusting though it is, may inflict less suffering than gin traps. Wherever it has reduced the rabbit population to less than 10 per cent we may be able to control the residue by such methods as gassing, and so actually abolish the gin. I would rather that 90 per cent of our rabbits died painfully of myxomatosis now than that year after year a proportion of them—amounting to a much greater total—should endure the appalling agony and terror of the trap. If the humanitarians would think about it *calmly* I believe they would agree.

MEANWHILE, the rabbit has disappeared completely from large areas of the English countryside: I doubt if there is a rabbit within ten miles of me as I write this. In my neighbour's cornfield, which I can see from my window, the oats grow tall right up to the headland; the year before last they were nibbled down for about 20 yards out from the hedges, and he lost, out of 15 acres, about 4 acres of corn. Small farms on the hill, which previously were able to support 75 sheep, now carry flocks of 100. The grass is lush at the woodsides where it used to be sick and sour from the rabbits' fouling.

Of course the rabbit's extinction is bound to have some effects on the flora and fauna. We may indeed lose a few rare flowers, smothered by the great growth of herbage; and the buzzards, which feed largely on rabbits, will probably retreat from some of the Cotswold hills which recently they recolonised. The foxes *may* become a little bolder; though rabbits have never provided their main source of food, for they eat great numbers of voles, rats, mice and frogs. The farmers suspect them of killing lambs, which I am sure they do occasionally, though marauding dogs are the likelier culprits. However, the loss of a lamb or two gives our farmers the excuse to organise fox-shoots, to the great annoyance of old-fashioned hunting-people and Masters of Fox-hounds. They do not really fear that fox-shooting will spoil their own sport; they know there are too many foxes, and that they are likely to have better hunting when the foxes are thinned out. But they regard it, still, as a social crime to shoot a fox: it is like the breaking of a taboo. The Colonel, between the wars, cared nothing for this taboo, and being driven hopping mad by the foxes which raided his pedigree poultry he took out his gun and shot three cubs which came out of his cornfield as it was being harvested. The M.F.H., who until that time had been his closest friend, *never spoke to him again*. They had been at Eton together, at Magdalen together, had ridden, soldiered, shot, fished, and drunk port together. But in the eyes of the M.F.H. the Colonel had committed the unforgivable sin. *He had shot a fox in his friend's hunting country*. He would have been forgiven almost anything else, I think, by those stiff-necked absurd hunting-people. He could have run away with somebody else's wife and they would have excused it, he could have thrown woodcocks in aspic at waiters at the annual hunt ball and they would have put it down to sportin' high spirits, he could have peppered a beater out shooting and they'd have thought little of it. But he hadn't shot a beater, he'd shot a fox, and so had defied a convention which was stricter than the statutory law. Moreover he had set a bad example to smallholders, little farmers, Saturday-afternoon gunners, idle poaching fellows, anybody who had a gun. " Mark my words, Sir, it isn't a question of one fox, or two foxes, or three. It's the *Principle* involved! Once you start muckin' about with Principles, where does it lead you? To anarchy, Sir! To Bolshevism, Sir! To the Barricades! "

OF COURSE the Saturday-afternoon gunner and the idle poaching fellow is very unlikely to waste a cartridge on a fox: when he lets off that sixpennorth of gunpowder he does so in the expectation of bagging something he can eat. And I imagine very few people have been tempted to eat a fox; the only one I have heard of was a sporting Rector of Solihull, Warwickshire, who lived in the 1820's. His pack of hounds having lost a particularly elusive fox after a very long run, he swore that if it was ever caught he'd cook it for dinner. It *was* caught, and His Reverence served it roasted to a convivial company on a great silver dish in his dining-room at Solihull Rectory.

But my poaching friends, Pistol, Bardolph and Nym, have less courage in this respect than the Rector. The foxes are safe from them; but I am afraid they sorely miss the few rabbits that they used to ferret out of the hedges on |Sunday. They miss the sport as well as the rabbit-stew; and I expect they miss the company of their ferrets, sly slinking creatures like themselves, which are certainly not worth keeping nowadays. During the war (when rabbits were fetching 15/- a couple!) a good ferret sold for two or three pounds. I doubt if you'd get a bob for one to-day—which is just half what I paid for a ferret during the slump of 1930. The circumstances of this purchase were unusual. I sold it to myself. Being then articled to my uncle, who was an auctioneer, I had at last been promoted from clerk to salesman. A ten-pound licence was bought on my behalf and one day I stood up in Elmbury Market to sell the "Poultry and Sundries", an assortment of boiling hens (2/- each if they were fat ones), goslings, a farmer's daughter's rabbit, puppy-dogs, pea-sticks, old implements, and unwanted rubbish of all kinds. Trembling and sweating with terror, I mounted the rostrum, which was an upturned apple-box, and offered Lot 1: a fitcher ferret. Nobody bid. Five shillings? Four? Three shillings then? Three shillings meant a lot in those days to the kind of idle poaching fellows who could do with a dark-coloured ferret (less visible on the rabbit bury than a white one, if the farmer came along!) So in vain I poured forth words most prodigally in praise of this bedraggled and wretched-looking creature, for it would be a shame and a disgrace to me, I supposed, if I failed to sell the very first lot I had ever offered by auction. Whatever little skill in language I then possessed was lavished upon the worthless animal, I described it in the terms by which poets have flattered their mistresses; Pericles, Demosthenes, Cicero, strove no more rhetorically than I; I spoke with the tongues of men and of angels, and all to no avail, for I did not get a single bid for the grubby little beast whose furtive and resentful eyes stared at me out of the wire cage. Finally in despair I put in a bid myself and bought it for 2/-; it repaid me for my flights of fancy with such ingratitude as the poets' mistresses have often shown them—it bit me clean through the thumb on the way home.

XI

IT always surprises me that the young are not more cynical than they are, since disillusion is their lot from early childhood to late 'teens. I am thinking particularly of the small patch of garden set aside by fond foolish parents " for the children's very own ". It is a patch, of course, stony and infertile, hedged round and perpetually shaded by privet-bushes; but " it will do for the children and it might teach them something." It does, oh, it does! A sixpenny packet of Shirley poppies provides the first lesson. They look so pretty in the picture on the packet. How different from the reality when a few attenuated plants come up, patchy and scattered because of the children's inexperience in shaking seed out of packets and because of the modesty of innumerable cats. But never mind. Let us try radishes, for children are surprisingly utilitarian in their outlook, and it greatly appeals to them to grow something which they can eat. And who could resist the crisp carmine-and-white in the picture on that first packet of radish-seed! I shall never forget it, for my particular sort was called French Breakfast, and I thought how wise were the French to begin their day with such a dish. What great if inglorious artist, I wonder, what Rubens, what Rembrandt of the radishes, set up those three little vegetables before him and painted the masterpiece which a small boy felt he could actually *nibble* if he liked! What was he paid for his piece of inspired humbug with which, in bitterness and anger, I compared the horrid reality when I pulled a bunch of radishes in order that I might indulge in a delicious French Breakfast at last? Instead of being round, they were tenuous as worms; and they were the colour of worms; and instead of being crisp they were as flaccid as worms. So much for the world's promises, I said, as I threw them away.

As a rule the dream blown away on the winds of disillusion is gone for ever; you might as well try to call the thistledown back to the thistlehead! But in this case the miracle *can* be accomplished, by a visit to the Village Flower Show. Brensham Flower Show does indeed restore the faith which I lost between the privet-bushes at the age of ten; for here the childhood dream comes true, and the painters of the pictures on the packet receive at long last their exoneration and acquittal. Indeed, those poor maligned artists, far from exaggerating, are shown to have done *less* than justice to their subjects; my neighbour's radishes are the colour of new-painted pillar-boxes, his carrots like the flesh of a salmon cut in two in a coloured advertisement for tinned salmon, his parsnips —which he spent three days digging out of the hard ground, using a teaspoon to remove the soil from the delicate tip as he approached the Antipodes,—his parsnips could never be cribb'd, cabin'd and confin'd in a seed-packet picture, they would need a full-length canvas at the very least. And those cauliflowers white and tight as snowballs between their trimmed green leaves, those tomatoes pristine as the new ball which our cricket-team can so rarely afford nowadays, those dahlias as big as dinner-plates, those chrysanthe-mums touched surely by Midas—they are the truth that is stranger than fiction, they were never seen upon any seed-packet in the world!

I do not presume to know how anybody managed to grow them. I have heard that in preparation for the planting of parsnips and carrots deep holes are bored with crowbars, as a man might drill for oil; I have heard that the contents of a whole cattle-yard, very nearly, were lavished upon the plants which bore those cricket-ball tomatoes; I have indeed heard whispered the false accusation which runs round the Flower Show every year, that my neighbour's cauliflowers were not his own after all, but were sent to him in a registered package all the way from Cornwall. Indeed I am told that in the North Country, where they go in largely for leeks and where they take their Flower Shows, as they take their cricket, much more seriously than we Southerners do, the Committee makes a tour of all the entrants' gardens about a fortnight before the show. They inspect the leeks in the ground and then with a special instrument solemnly tattoo their leaves. This ensures that the leeks are really grown by him who submits them to the show and that he doesn't, when the show is over, sell his prize exhibits to his mate who has entered for another show in a neighbouring village!

But for my part I do not care who grew the things; for whatever garden they flourished in, it is certain that they came out of a seed-packet originally; and so after thirty years the painter of radishes and Virginia Stock is vindicated. My faith is restored, I am a cynic no longer. Hurray then for the Flower Show, refurbisher of dreams!

LIKE most Village Flower Shows, ours is concerned less with the Epicurean aspect than with the sheer bulk of the vegetables. The onions, for instance, make me think of the Ram of Derbyshire. The least of them you could place on the top of a pint mug and it would sit there like an egg in an egg-cup; the largest is not *very* far short of the size of a soccer ball.

These monsters, of course, were grown from the previous summer's bulbs; and having been so long a-growing they are as tough as horse-radishes. What are the things for? I suppose if you had the energy to sieve them into soup, and if you had eight hungry children who all liked onion-soup better than anything else in the world, you might manage to use up two or three a month during the winter. Otherwise they would come in handy as medicine-balls, to play with on the sands.

Far be it from me to blame the gardeners who win good prizes with these monstrosities; but I do think it is time that the horti-cultural societies who run the various flower shows took to giving prizes for edible onions. They have at last taken a stand against immense vegetable marrows and two-foot-long runner-beans; let them now turn their attention to onions and leeks.

Nobody wants to eat—and nobody could eat—a leek resembling a palm-tree such as Omar Khayyám with his wine, his book, his loaf of bread and his Thou, might have comfortably idled under in a desert oasis. So if we must have classes for these freaks of nature why not be frank about it and print the schedule as follows:—

CLASS

1.	LEEKS	(*Ornamental*)
2.	LEEKS	(*Edible*)
3.	ONIONS	(*Soup or Football*)
4.	ONIONS	(*Culinary*)

In the old days, of course, when the Squire's head gardener carried off all the prizes with his enormous vegetables, his yard-long carrots, his even longer parsnips, his 10 lb. cauliflowers and so on, it was the poor Squire who had to eat the things.

" Dish up the First Prize carrots for his Lordship's table, Alfred." But Alfred, and Martha and the butler and the head gardener himself, took jolly good care that the nice tasty little vegetables remained in the kitchen. It was they who dined like lords!

THE cult of size-rather-than-quality is not confined to vegetable gardeners. Zinnias get bigger every year, and soon, I expect, will have blooms as large as dahlias. As for the dahlias themselves, they now bear heads so heavy that the stems will not support them; they have to be tied up and propped up with a sort of wigwam of sticks and sheltered from the rain and wind by little tents or even old umbrellas.

The flower-beds of one of our dahlia-growers were planted last week with three old coloured parasols and a golfing-umbrella! It is magnificent, but it is not gardening. As for these huge blooms themselves, they seem to me to resemble nothing so much as coloured cabbages. If only one could eat them, they might be worth growing.

WHEN THE FLOWER SHOW is over our gardens are denuded and suddenly autumnal. Soon we shall begin digging up and planting again and even begin to look forward to another summer. Meanwhile all is death and decay—

> *Heavily hangs the broad sunflower*
> *Over its grave i' the earth so chilly:*
> *Heavily hangs the hollyhock,*
> *Heavily hangs the tiger-lily.*

Perversely, real gardeners delight in this season of cleaning-off and tidying up; for they are perfectionists who have learned by long experience that only in the preparation can they achieve perfection —never in the result. There will always be weeds, blights, droughts, puppies knocking over delphiniums, cats kicking up the seeds and making the rows crooked, which is anathema to gardeners, who love straight lines. I have read that the Chinese communists in Malaya, fighting from jungle hideouts, used to give away their positions to the Japanese airmen because they could not resist planting their vegetables in orderly rows; whether this was because they were good gardeners or simply good communists I do not know.

But I do know that all true gardeners (I am not one) are apostles of order and the sworn foes of anarchy. Their souls yearn for symmetry; even the fact that flowers of the same kind grow to unequal heights annoys them. The Duke of York's head gardener in *King Richard the Second* showed a typical mistrust of individuality when he said to his under-gardener:

> *Go thou, and like an executioner*
> *Cut off the heads of too fast growing sprays*
> *That look too lofty in our commonwealth:*
> *All must be even in our government.*

Of course it is impossible to achieve this equalitarian state in the summer, when every border becomes a hot-bed of anarchy; when you are never quite sure what weeds are coming up among the flowers, what secret convolvulus or sly sowthistle, what dandelion's plumy seeds are making parachute-landings unbeknownst in the borders; what grubs and slugs are multiplying unseen. But when the soil is bare and newly forked, then you can be certain that the devil's minions are at any rate temporarily vanquished. You have won a battle, if you haven't won a war.

THE OLD COLONEL had a gardener who was typical of all gardeners, and most properly he was called Adam. Between the Colonel and himself it was sometimes difficult to tell who was the boss. I once overheard him say in the pub: "I've got a good master. He lets I alone." It is by this yardstick of non-intervention that gardeners judge their employers; and I heard him upbraided for his use of that old-fashioned expression, "Master", by a smart young jackanapes who worked in a factory.

"Feudal," said the young jackanapes, having learned the word at school. "That's what your outlook is, Adam—feudal. Thank 'Eaven some of us 'ave grown out of that way of thinking."

I doubt if Adam knew what 'feudal' meant, but he quelled the young man, who happened to be his nephew, with a single sentence. He said simply: "Who be *thy* master, then?" And there was something in his tone which called up an endless vista of conveyor-belts and shop-stewards and foremen, anonymous managers, faceless, unknown directors, financiers, stockbrokers, banks.

The young man, knowing not whom he served nor what shareholders lived on the fruits of his labour, had nothing to say; and old Adam stalked out.

That was the only time I ever saw him ruffled; for he possessed the kind of patience which seems to be a perquisite of those who grow things and whose fortunes are bound up with the unpredictable seasons, the infinitely capricious English weather, and the slow, obstinate, inexorable forces of Nature.

Adam had the same shrug for the late frost which cut off his peaches, for the mysterious virus which shrivelled his scarlet snap-dragons just when the beds were at their best, for the summer drought and for the winter flood.

"These things," he used to say, "level themselves out in the end." That phrase summarises a whole philosophy, the gardener's and the farmer's philosophy of levelling-out.

It is founded, I think, upon an assumption that the weather is shared roughly between God and the Devil, with a slight advantage on the side of God. The Devil's armoury is reinforced by noisome insects, weeds, grubs, slugs and snails, mischievous birds, and various other ' pestses '. But God provides the antidote through benevolent birds, hedgehogs, other ' friends of man ' and, recently, by His revelation of the efficacy of D.D.T.

It sounds like a fatalistic philosophy, but if you examine it more closely you will see that it is the very opposite. For it assumes that the margin between the powers of Good and Evil, in so far as they affect the flower-beds and the vegetable-patch, is a very narrow one. The gardener is always at war, from the moment when he first picks up a spade to the time when the sexton picks up *his* spade to dig the hole in the churchyard. But by then, because of the Law of Levelling-out, a man of three-score-years-and-ten will have known some dozens of sweet seasons as well as some dozens of foul ones. *If he has worked hard enough to deserve it* he may have fulfilled his particular ambition. He may have achieved, for one season at least, a complete succession of well-matched colours in his herbaceous border. He may have attained the sort of horticultural immortality of having a daffodil or tulip or a new pippin named after him. He may even have won the Cup three times in succession at the local Flower Show.

Adam's battle-honours, in this long fight of his with the weather and the 'pestses' and the weeds, were displayed on a row of red, green and yellow cards tacked to the upper staging in his master's greenhouse; and on some more cards, faded and stained, in the green-houses of those previous masters whom he had served in turn until they died or left the village.

These were his battle-honours: Dahlias FIRST PRIZE; Hothouse Tomatoes FIRST PRIZE; Carrots, long, FIRST PRIZE; Narcissi, poeticus, FIRST PRIZE and GOLD MEDAL; Onions SECOND PRIZE; and so on. His own name, of course, did not appear on any of the cards; and when we read the list of prize-winners in the local paper we found no mention of Adam. It was the Colonel who had won that Special Award for chrysanths.

But this did not trouble Adam at all. He cherished his proud anonymity as do the private soldiers in famous regiments, who perform the hard fighting while their generals get most of the credit for it. "Everybody knows," he would say, "that *I* grew 'em." By 'everybody' he meant the whole population of a small village; and that was all that mattered to him, for his world was no wider than that. But you must not think that he lacked the spirit of independence nor a sense of his own personal dignity. He possessed more independence, really, than that young jackanapes, his nephew, who earned twice as much as Adam did, for bashing out the mudguards of motor-cars. A long time ago, in 1926, when Adam was working for the Colonel, there was, you probably remember, a General Strike.

Now, Adam, of course, belonged to no union, but he was a Radical in politics, and he always voted Labour, because there were no real Radicals left. He had to decide, therefore, where his loyalty lay; and the conflict in his mind must have been painful indeed, since there is always a great deal of important work to be done in the garden in early May. On the morning of the strike, however, he absented himself from the Colonel's garden. For a week or so he remained wretchedly at home, doing his duty according to his lights but thinking of the runner-beans that ought to be planted, the early potatoes that ought to be moulded, the bedding plants that ought to be put out, the peas that ought to be hoed. At last the unions gave in, and Stanley Baldwin told them: " The strike will end forthwith—that means immediately."

Forthwith and immediately Adam hobbled up to the Colonel's and began to plant his runner-beans. The Colonel walked out into the vegetable garden, noticed him, and passed the time of day. He said nothing about the strike; nor did Adam. A perfect mutual courtesy manifested itself. The Colonel said:

" We'll have to think about sticking those sweet peas." And Adam replied without a blink of an eyelid, in a tone which suggested that the Colonel and he were equally to blame:

" Aye, master; we be late sticking they sweet peas." And that was the end of that.

How pleasant it would be if all industrial relations could be carried on as sensibly and with as good manners!

Adam was about sixty then; he died in his seventy-third year, within a month or two of the Colonel. The last time I saw him was in the autumn before the war. I talked to him over the hedge as he cleaned off the herbaceous border, forked between the Michaelmas daisies, and cut down the dead hollyhocks. He finished the job and straightened himself stiffly, feeling at last the burden of his years. " Looks nice, don't it? " he said, surveying the freshly turned earth in all the flower-borders, not a single weed to be seen.

" It'll look nicer," I ventured, " in the spring."

" Maybe." But he looked unconvinced. I dare say when a man is seventy-three the winter seems longer and the ultimate spring less sure. Perhaps some such thought was passing through old Adam's mind. If so, I do not think it dismayed him, for the immortal rhythm of mortal things—the growing, the fading, the dying, the rebirth—had drummed itself into his consciousness till he knew himself to be part of it. The churchyard was the accepted, inevitable, undreaded journey's end.

As he stood admiring his tidy brown borders he struck me as a man entirely at peace. He was untroubled by doubt or fear or hatred (save that, of course, he hated weeds and grubs, which is much better than hating Russians or Americans or one's next-door neighbour.) He was contented with an imperfect world in which rain and sunshine, bad seasons and good, were eternally " levelling themselves out in the end." Yet, knowing its imperfection, he felt no bewilderment about the point and purpose of it all. How many of us can say as much for ourselves?

XII

Walking through High Beech Wood as the leaves fall, I observe some mummified bundles of feather and fur hanging from the hazel-twigs at the place where three rides meet: two crows like black and midnight hags, a skeleton jay with its blue cheek-feathers still incongruously sticking to its bare skull, a couple of weasels, an attenuated stoat, some little owls and a hawk whose proud head and aquiline beak like some ancient Roman's seem to scorn the very blowflies that buzz about it.

By these gruesome tokens, to which now and then he adds a new victim, Old Henry demonstrates that he is still the petty lord and tyrant over all that runs or flies in High Beech Wood. This old keeper is like a ghost from the past, and his world is as dead as his victims on the gibbet; the Squire who was his master is buried in the churchyard and the Squire's son who would have inherited High Beech is buried by the drifting sands of Libya, and the shooting is now owned by a syndicate from the city. They took over Henry with the shoot, mainly because he occupied the gamekeeper's cottage and could not lawfully be turned out; so although he is over eighty, he still walks the woodland paths he walked in his vigorous youth, still carries his old hammer-gun under his arm (though he rarely shoots anything with it), still sets his snares and gins in the runs which he knows as well as a townsman knows the streets of his own town.

His ears are still sharp enough to hear the fox's bark or the jay's warning screech or the twig cracked by a poacher's boot a hundred yards away; his eyes, bleared and misty with the years, can still spot the hovering hawk or the tell-tale empty cartridge-case in the ride or the broken bracken-frond where an intruder has passed by. Out of long habit he still wages war against his lifetime's foes— magpie and jay, hawk and owl, stoat, weasel, fox and half-wild cat, and those two-legged varmints, as he calls them, who sneak through the wood with their lurcher dogs on Saturday afternoons and Sundays. But there are few real poachers nowadays, and I think Old Henry secretly misses them. " Bless you, in the days before the war " (he means the 1914 war, of course) " they used to make a business of it, working in gangs, half a dozen of the varmints banded together." From time to time, he will tell you, the gangs shot it out with the keepers in the dark wood at midnight, and once Old Henry tracked a man home to his cottage by the blood-trail from his wounded leg! Foggy nights in winter were the most dangerous; for then the poachers brought their guns into the wood to shoot roosting pheasants, hoping the sound would be mistaken for the fog-signals on the nearby railway line. Those were the days! " Why, master, I minds how in my dad's time, when he keepered here for Squire's father, they used to set *man-traps* at the edge of the wood; and Dad used to tell us how he once heard a varmint squealing in one, just as a trapped rabbit squeals. . . ."

One of the things that mark out Henry as an anachronism is his tremendous sense of the sanctity of private property. It always strikes me as a little strange that he who has never owned any land himself—who indeed has never owned anything save a hammer-gun, a few pounds' worth of furniture, half a dozen pullets and a fat pig—should guard so jealously the rights of his masters, who probably care very little about those rights anyhow. Picnickers at holiday-seasons, bluebell-pickers, even lovers playing their age-old games among the bracken, always stir Henry into a furious rage and he yells at them: " Don't you know this is private property? Didn't you see the notice-board? Don't you know you're tres-passing? " Then perhaps some pert wench—even girls seem to know the law nowadays—pipes up with " Trespassers *can't* be prosecuted—said so on the wireless—so there! " and Old Henry, who has no book-learning, shuffles away discomfited. The law was different, surely, in the old Squire's day!

On the first shooting day he puts on his best pair of breeches, as he has done every October for sixty years—before that he didn't possess a best pair—and goes down to the main road to meet the guns. He touches his cap to the syndicate men just as he used to touch it to the Squire and the parson and their Lordships and the young gentlemen on leave from the Indian Army; but he no longer knows their names, nor, it seems, do they often remember his, for there are too many names to remember if you live in London-town. He leads them down to the first drive and shows them to their places, each marked with a piece of folded newspaper in a cleft stick; then he goes off to take charge of the beaters, who seem much more tiresome and unruly than beaters used to be—the boys sometimes cheek him, even the older men no longer treat him with the respect due to a Head Keeper;—alas, there are no underkeepers now! However, he keeps the rag-tag-and-bobtail lot in line somehow, keeps them tapping on the trees and shouting " Yi-yi-yi! " and because he's known the wood ever since he could walk he drives the pheasants straight and high and never fails to show the guns a good day's sport. When it is over he bundles up the birds and counts them and hands them out to the guests, touching his cap as he does so, just the same as in the Squire's day. But then it used to be:

" A cock and a hen each for the young gentlemen, Henry; and a brace of cocks for the vicar; and don't forget to take a brace each to all the tenants and to send three brace down to the cottage hospital."

Somehow it's different now. The head of the syndicate, counting up the bag, turns to his friends and says " Not bad. That's sixty-two at two pounds a brace! "—and there are none for the farmers and none for the hospital, for the way to run a week-end shoot, thinks the head of the syndicate, is to have your sport *and* show a bit of profit at the end of the season!

Henry takes his tip and touches his cap and hobbles back through

the dusky wood collecting up the cleft marker-sticks on his way:
a shadow among the shadows, a relic of the past.

One day as I walked along the ride I found by chance a tightly-
folded wad of newspaper that had somehow survived the weathers
in the hollow of an old tree. It was one of those bits of paper
which Henry wedges into the cleft sticks; I unfolded it, and was
astonished to find myself reading a report of the Coronation of
King George the Fifth! They had better paper then, and better
printing ink, I dare say; and the old Squire, apparently, used nothing
less substantial than copies of *The Times* to mark the positions of
his guns. I walked on, and when I encountered Henry wandering
round the woodside with his spaniel (which is almost as stiff in its
joints as he is) I told him what I had found.

"1911?" he repeated. I don't know how much or how
little the date meant to him, but it carried him back into the past.
"1911? Ah, those were the days. . . . Old Squire used to put
down two thousand pheasants then . . . never shot less than two
hundred brace on the opening day. We used to drive 'em over
the valley down there. Squire said he liked to have 'em looking
no bigger'n starlings. There was a greenhouse on t'other side of
the valley and 'twas Squire's dearest wish to drop a bird on it and
smash the glass. "A fiver for you, Henry," he used to say, "if
you can put a bird over me so high that he falls slap in the middle
of that greenhouse!" And one day Squire did it. Pleased as
punch, he was, couldn't have been more pleased if he'd come into
a fortune. I had my fiver and it cost him another pound to mend
the greenhouse glass. But, bless you, sovereigns was nothing to
the gentry in those days. They'd have a ten pound sweep on
who shot the first woodcock; and the winner would pick up a
hundred or two. We keepers used to like that; it meant an extra
tip for us if the gent who won was open-fisted."

Wages were low then—Henry thought himself lucky to get
fifty pounds a year and a decent cottage—but tips were frequent
and generous. Nobody gave less than a fiver if the bag amounted
to more than a hundred brace; or if they did they were not invited

again! One guest, Henry remembers, was so remarkably mean that he slipped away without tipping at all; but it was the keeper's duty to clean and pack up the guns and Henry conveniently forgot to put them on the train. In due course the mean man wrote to his host, asking for the return of his pair of Purdeys, and the Squire, who well understood the situation, wrote back regretting the delay, adding a pointed PS.:

"I never interfere with my keepers. *Perhaps you will get in touch with Henry?*"

A five-pound note arrived by return, and Henry sent off the guns with his humble apologies.

So Henry babbled on, as old men do, until a jay's screech called him back from the past suddenly and he picked up his gun, which must be older than himself, and touched his cap, and hobbled off into the wood. "Well, I must be getting on with it . . . must chivvy up they troublesome jays." A little later I heard a shot; and so I dare say the hawk and the owl, the weasels and the draggled crows, have new company on the gallows. There they swing from the hazel-twigs, dancing their dance of death whenever the wind blows, clicketty-clack when skeleton meets skeleton, old dry bones jigging together. And now the jay swings with them, and the flies buzz about it, and if you happen to pass downwind of the gallows-tree you will catch a whiff that used to identify the place to all who went by it, a mouldering whiff that belongs like Henry to the dead past.

XIII

B<small>UT</small> H<small>ENRY</small>'s gallows won't survive much longer; they have begun to cut down the trees in High Beech Wood. Already the syndicate has sold most of the timber in the park and the best of the oaks in the hedgerows. Now they are starting on the beeches.

I never cease to be appalled by the rate at which we are destroying our heritage of trees. I am not thinking of the normal felling of mature woodlands (for trees must be harvested even as corn) but of the casual, haphazard and entirely wanton slaughter of good trees in field and park, hedgerow and avenue, at streamside and roadside. Recently we have lost, in my own neighbourhood, a clump of immemorial elms, a row of roadside oaks, two monumental walnuts—and in each case there was no *reason* for the felling except perhaps the owner's greed. That, and our strange, new, un-English passion for tidiness: if a tree happens to get in the way of somebody's pet plan for making the landscape look as suburban as possible, down it comes.

Hedgerow timber, which used to be one of the glories of our land, is fast disappearing; farmers hate it, and the old-fashioned landlords who used to reward their hedge-cutters with a shilling for every good sapling they left would be regarded as crazy by our modern get-rich-quicks. Housing, and the outward spread of the towns, costs us many more trees than it need; for the planners of the housing estates usually lay everything flat before they start, because it is expedient to do so, though with the exercise of a little ingenuity they could incorporate many of the existing trees in their layout. Indeed, I have lately come to the conclusion that the urban-minded actually *dislike* trees and regard them as an unnecessary nuisance. I know of one case where the occupants of some new Council-houses petitioned the Local Authority for the removal of an oak-tree which had been left standing; they said it interfered with their view, which consisted of a main road upon which buses and lorries passed all day. And I read somewhere of another petition, for the removal of a tree in a newly-built square on the grounds that it was the nightly perch of a barn-owl, whose hooting disturbed the inhabitants of the district!

WE USED, in the countryside at any rate, to *respect* good trees; they were the familiar landmarks with which we grew up; a landlord or Council, cutting down a notable tree, would be extremely unpopular in consequence. But nowadays, I think, we have lost the *corporate* sense of property, the feeling that a great oak, say, is something in which we all have a share, that it is not just Smith's oak or Jones's oak but yours and mine. It is a curious paradox that when private property was most sacrosanct, two or three generations ago, and when the landowner possessed absolute power to do whatever he liked with his own land, he rarely used that power wantonly; indeed he would often plant a spinney, or preserve an existing one, simply for the sake of the ' view '—not his own ' view ' only, but that of everybody in the neighbourhood. To-day, the owner of a property hardly ever takes into consideration the feelings of his neighbours; and this is particularly true, I think, of urban people who come into possession of trees. Either they don't like being ' shaded ', or they believe the trees ' harbour creepy-crawlies ', or they fear that the roots will interfere with their wonderful plans for making a fortune out of growing early vegetables under cloches; or perhaps they merely want to make a new garden according to their own ideas. This last, at any rate, is a natural ambition for anybody who has just come into possession of a piece of land; and in the old days it did not have such disastrous consequences, because by the time the new owner had laid about him with an axe for two or three days, or hired some men to do the job and seen what a mess they were making, he was apt to have second thoughts and to modify his programme of destruction. But nowadays he simply rings up the contractor, who arrives with a bulldozer, and in a couple of hours the job is done: *irrevocably*.

THE FARMERS themselves are much to blame for the unnecessary felling which is beginning to make some parts of the countryside look rather like a prairie. A Bank Manager told me the other day that many of the farmers who come to him for loans seem to regard their standing timber as liquid assets which can be turned into cash immediately. " Suppose a young man wants to buy a farm with the aid of a mortgage, and he can't quite raise the balance of the purchase-price, he will say ' There's plenty of timber; I'll cash in straight away on the trees.' " I wonder what sharp lesson will teach the farmers that trees aren't just a jolly decoration on the landscape, a bit of ' natural beauty ' which people like me are always blathering about, to be destroyed if it gets in the way or if its destruction brings in enough ready cash to pay the rent for one year?

Recently, at the end of a dry spell, a great wind smote the east coast of England; spring cultivations had been done, crops had been planted, and the soil no doubt was in that friable state which is the farmers' pride. The wind, however, bore away this top-soil and according to some reports produced ' a thick dust-fog ' so that motorists had to use their windscreen-wipers. Some of the crops blew away with the soil; whole fields of beet, (which was just coming through,) were lifted and scattered by the wind. The Fen farmers, interviewed by the newspaper-men, sounded surprised as well as hurt by this phenomenon. Possibly they put it down to atom-tests in Nevada. They didn't, as far as I know, put it down to the absence of trees.

Why on earth don't the Ministry of Agriculture and the National Farmers' Union tell the farmers in capital letters that even in this moist climate TREES AND HEDGES ARE NECESSARY TO HUSBANDRY? Everywhere I go nowadays I see trees being cut down (and hardly ever replaced) and hedges being grubbed up because they are 'unnecessary', 'expensive to trim and lay' or 'a waste of space which might be growing something useful'. But perhaps the market-gardeners of Evesham and of Wisbech, where you can't see a tree for miles, will discover one day that hedges *were* useful, when their spring onions and their radishes or half the ridging round their potatoes blow away in 'a thick dust-fog' in a dry spring!

THE GROWERS of Evesham seem to me to be among the worst offenders. When I drive from my home to catch the London train I am shocked afresh, almost every week, by the destruction of hedgerows, and even where the hedges remain, of perfectly harmless hedgerow trees. Sometimes the destruction is quite pointless. In one place, for instance, there used to be a long row of sallows, 'sallies' as we call them, growing not even in a field but along a wide grass verge. They were a pleasant landmark along a dreary road and the children used to collect their 'palms' at Easter, and these 'palms' also gave a useful early feed to the bees which were hungry after the long winter. Apart from that the sallows supported a fairly large population of useful insects and were probably nesting-places for a few sorts of insect-eating birds. It could have been no conceivable advantage to the farmer (or the Highway authority—I don't know which was responsible) to have them down. It cost the labour of a couple of men for a few days, plus the use of some expensive machinery. *Why* grub them up, then? I can only assume that some farmers have a sort of vague unformulated grievance against trees; or that the Highway authority has the queer modern passion for 'tidiness', which is represented nowadays by neat suburban-looking verges upon which nothing grows except the dutiful grasses.

IF YOU want to know what agricultural England was like before such vandals got to work on it, go to an Art Gallery and take a look at a landscape by Constable or Gainsborough. You will be astonished at the lushness and the green shade of it all; the sense of drowsy summer heat mitigated by the cool of hedge and spinney; the scattered oaks and elms beneath which the cattle stand and seem almost to flick their tails, they come so alive for you; the pool in which horses stand fetlock deep, or dip their velvet noses to send the circle of ripples running out.

" Look here upon this picture and on this ". . . . If you could identify that same pastoral scene to-day, you wouldn't recognise it. The scattered trees cut down (they were ' in the way '); the hedge-row that was once milky with may grubbed up (an electric fence will do instead); the pond itself filled in, probably, in the interests of good drainage.

We think we are very clever to make all these ' improvements '; but one day, as in Lincolnshire, a chill wind begins to blow. *Whoosh!* And we who in a sense sowed it reap the whirlwind.

XIV

SINCE most agricultural tenancies end at Michaelmas, September is the busiest month for the auctioneers. It is also the heyday of Henry Higgins. You may meet him anywhere on the road which leads to a sale of furniture or farming stock, and you may recognise him by the legend stencilled neatly on the side of his smart dray: "MR. H. HIGGINS, BRENSHAM, GNL. DLR." That "Mr." is significant; it is part of his personal dignity, he has a handle to his name! He is proud, independent, individualist; a free man, as he often declares, in a free country. His dignity is implicit too in the shine on his mare's harness and on his own boots and leggings: the sort of shine that is only achieved by elbow-grease. It is as if he were aware that he is certainly the best-known person for twenty miles around, not excluding lords and ladies, and must therefore keep up appearances. Also, there is more to an auction-sale than a bargain and a haggle: it is a minor social occasion, at which a man is liable to encounter a score of old friends. So Mr. Higgins wears his best bowler-hat and a pair of grey breeches rather widely cut out of good cloth by a country tailor who understands the complex sociology of breeches—which have their hierarchies, being shaped with a slight but perceptible difference for various sorts of customers, farmer, vet, dealer, gamekeeper, stable-boy and squire.

There is a look in Mr. Higgins's eye, as he jogs towards a sale, which reminds me of the huntsman going to the meet or the angler setting off to the river: a look of happy and eager anticipation, as if to say "I wonder what sport we shall have this morning." If he had been born into a different station, he might have become a big-game hunter, collecting ' heads ', or perhaps a seeker-out of rare china or curios; for he is one of those fortunate people for whom the whole of life is an endless and exciting quest, and in a sense he is luckier than the connoisseur or the shikar because the area of his quest is so much wider than theirs. There is a limit to the diversity of beasts and beautiful china; but the objects of Mr. Higgins's pursuit are as infinitely various as the whims and activities of mankind, ranging from " a nice li'l quiet cob suitable for a young lady " to " a coupla fitcher ferrets for the keeper, a ton or two of perry pears, a pig-tro', a wardrobe small enough to go up Mrs. Robinson's winding staircase, a good lurcher pup for old Manasseh next time the gipsies come round, half a dozen boiling hens, a nanny-goat in milk, some galvanised sheets and a sitting of goose-eggs."

I firmly believe that there is nothing in the world he would not buy if he thought the price was right; for his whole life is founded upon a kind of magpie philosophy expressed in four words " 'Twill come in handy." A large orchard behind his house, transformed into a rural slum with fowl-houses, chicken-runs, rabbit-hutches, pigstyes and sheds, bears witness to the practical application of his philosophy. Piled haphazard in the sheds are iron bedsteads, old chairs, harness, pothampers, odd fragments of broken machinery, cartwheels, implements, drainpipes and sheer junk of every description, all acquired and hoarded on the principle that some day, in circumstances however remote and improbable, these things will come in handy. And sure enough they do. Farmer Dudfield has the misfortune to break some intricate part of the mechanism of his binder at harvest-time, and not even Briggs the blacksmith can fix it; so he takes it along to Mr. Higgins, who stares at it for a long time and ' scrats his yud ' and says at last: " I minds I bought an old binder at the Manor Farm sale five years come Michaelmas, and if thee'll help me shift them bits of old bicycles I reckon we'll find her at the back of 'em; and then we'll see if the pieces match up." Or it may be a question of a ball-cock for a cistern when a catastrophe happens to the Rector's plumbing; or a hurricane-lamp or a whetstone or a draining-rod or any of the hundred and one things which feckless countrymen, living far from shops, are apt to need in a hurry. Whatever it is, the chances are that Mr. Higgins will be able to provide it out of his 40 years' accumulation if only you give him time to scrat his yud and puzzle out where it may be: which he does by a process of complicated mnemonics: "Now old Matthew Dyer pegged out the day war started; but his sale wasn't till Lady Day. And I bought that pony-trap from a gipsy on the way back from his sale, so if we look *behind* the pony-trap we ought to come across the horse-clippers I gave a quid for at Matthew Dyer's. . . ."

Hardly a day goes by but yields fresh evidence in support of Mr. Higgins's cherished theory about the ultimate handiness of things. Not long ago he bought an ancient Brougham from a man he disliked, who was subsequently very boastful of the fact that he'd got rid of his museum-piece for thirty shillings. But within a few months Mr. Higgins had sold the two front wheels for a pound apiece, and the top for fifteen shillings " to make a summerhouse " —of all strange improvisations!—and a year later, when the previous owner of the Brougham asked him if he had such a thing as a hand-cart, Mr. Higgins knocked one together out of two packing-cases and fitted it with the rear wheels of the vehicle, for which he took pleasure in charging exactly thirty bob.

I have said that Mr. Higgins will buy anything; but there is one recurrent item in the sale catalogues about which he is hesitant and for which in no circumstances will he bid more than a shilling: " Books *in lots*." " I tells you frankly," he said to me once. " I'm *frightened* of books." He is afraid of them because he doesn't understand them; they are probably the only things in the catalogue upon which he cannot accurately put a value. He has heard that there are old books worth thousands of pounds, and this thought makes him unhappy every time a heap of nineteenth-century litera-ture is offered for sale. He kicks the heap in a tentative and half-contemptuous way, turning the books over with his foot and cocking a puzzled eye at the calf-bound volume of Sermons and the *History of Animated Nature* by Oliver Goldsmith; would these, perhaps, be worth thousands of pounds? "Come along, gentlemen," says the auctioneer. "Who'll offer me half a crown? Nobody? Put the next lot with 'em, then." And after a long pause there comes a kind of agonised groan from Mr. Higgins, as if the reluctant bid were dragged painfully out of him against his will: " A bob."

So the temperance tracts and the unreadable poems and the cheap editions of Dickens make a mildewed pile in one of his leaky sheds, and Mr. Higgins shakes his head every time he glances at them: " I'm frit of books, Mister, and that's the truth of it." But one day, as I sorted among the heap to humour him, I came across a battered exercise-book, written in a prim, severe and somehow chilly hand. It seemed at first to contain nothing but names and dates, set out in meticulous columns; but as I turned over the pages I discovered that the book was a record of the comings and goings of servants, kept as one might keep a herd-book by some cold great lady at a time when servants were plentiful and ladies hard to please.

" *Green, Priscilla,*" I read. " *Kitchenmaid, Aged* 16. *Dismissed for gross misconduct. See Wilkins, James.*"

I turned the page:

" *Wilkins, James. Under footman. Aged* 19. *Dismissed for gross misconduct. See Green, Priscilla.*"

I perceived then that the faded brown copperplate writing had a tale to tell, if only a man could read it, and I said to Mr. Higgins: " I'll give you half a crown for this." I swear that in 40 years of dealing he had never looked startled before, he had never committed the fatal *faux-pas*, unheard of in huckstering men, the self-betrayal, the unspoken admission that the price offered was greater than the price expected. " Half a *crown*? " he gasped; and then to cover up his solecism he added swiftly: " But of course, they're not up my street, books ain't; I'm frit of 'em."

As complex as his store-keeping is Mr. Higgins's private and unique system of accountancy. Among people he knows well he is curiously reluctant to deal for cash; it is an affront to his dignity to offer him half a crown. " 'Twill square itself up in the end," he says airily, and makes a note of the debt in smudgy indelible pencil on the inside flap of a cigarette-packet. At the end of the day he adds the packet to his collection, which he keeps in a deep drawer, and six months later, on a wet Sunday, he sorts them out, deciphers the mysterious hieroglyphs, and proceeds as he puts it " to do his money." This is a very painful labour; and all day long he sucks the indelible pencil until his mouth looks like a clown's and his hands like the hands of a blackberry-picker; but at last the task is done, and next morning the postman brings you an involved but absolutely accurate statement, running perhaps something like this:

Mr. . . . . in account with Mr. H. Higgins.

To chain for bike	2 6		*contra*	
„ lamp for ditto	3 0	Cider apples	1 0 0	
„ helping at pig		Sprout plants		5 6
killing	5 0	Withy poles		3 0
„ 2 boltins straw	1 6	Rabbits bt. from		
„ half hogsyud cask	16 0	young Miss	10 0	
„ old iron furnace				
for boiling up	gratis			
„ horse-rug, worn	10 6			
	£1 18 6		£1 18 6	

The figures at the bottom of the second column are written with an almost triumphant flourish, as if to say " There you are; I told you so; it squares itself up in the end! "

I do not pretend to know how the economics of his extraordinary business work out; for no chartered accountant (and certainly no Income Tax inspector!) ever sets eyes on Mr. Higgins's drawerful of old Player's packets, and it would plainly be impossible for anybody to estimate the value of those heaps of odds-and-ends which fill the tumbledown sheds from floor to roof. Indeed they have no real value, only a hypothetical one based on the assumption that some day, somehow, they will come in handy. Who would have thought that the piles of old iron which before the war made a sort of Magnetic Mountain at the bottom of Mr. Higgins's orchard would be worth as many pounds in 1950 as they were worth shillings ten years before? And who would have thought that the American Negro soldiers who camped near the village in 1943 would turn out to be devoted, and indeed maniacal, bicyclists at a time when bicycles could not be had in the shops for love or money? For weeks on end Mr. Higgins was to be seen in his orchard matching wheels to frames, hammering out bent forks and handlebars, fitting together, screwing together, even tying together the wrecks he had bought twenty years ago for a song; and round and round the village green tore the chocolate coons on Mr. Higgins's bicycles, hugely grinning at the amazed village girls, and only grinning the broader if a front wheel happened to fly off at full speed. Thus Mr. Higgins's little fortune is founded upon imponderable chances and unforeseeable things.

During the war the heaps of junk in his orchard gradually dwindled away. First the old iron went, then the timber, then the bicycles, and then, miraculously it must have seemed to him, the books, which were bought by a wastepaper merchant for two pounds the lot. ("I was glad to see them go," said Mr. Higgins with huge relief. "I was glad to be shut of them.") Then for a time his business contracted, as the range of things which could be bought and sold without a licence became more limited; bureaucrats and inspectors troubled him, but he brushed them off as one brushes off flies, confounding them by his splendid *confessio fidei:* "I'm a free man; and this is a free country." His wallet waxed fat despite them; nor did his run of good fortune end with the war. In 1946, prompted by some prescience (for he has his ear close to the ground, like the gipsies with whom he is friendly and whose huckstering blood, it is said, runs in his veins,) he returned for a space to his old trade of horse-coping. He bought half a dozen rough and shaggy cobs to graze in his orchard, and half a dozen more to put out to tack; and all the wise people who were busily applying for supplementary petrol coupons thought he had gone off his head. Then came the autumnal crisis, and the suspension of the basic ration; and within a fortnight he had sold all his cobs, all his long-stored sets of harness, reins, horse-collars, pony-traps, governess-cars, and indeed any old vehicle which could conceivably be pulled by a horse.

But that was the end of the seller's market. Prices began to fall, and at last Mr. Higgins is beginning to stock up again. Two or three times a week he jogs off in his dray to the sales of furniture and farm-stock, and returns at evening with his assorted load of wheels, hencoops, cider-barrels, broken lawn-mowers, rusty implements, sticks of furniture, half a dozen bantams for the Rector's lady, some guinea-pigs which he bought because nobody else would bid for them. . . . Yet although he is as smart, as important-looking, as alert and dignified as ever, there can be no doubt about it that Mr. Higgins is growing old. The burden of the years begins to show itself in an increasing selectiveness; he who was as acquisitive as a magpie has become almost choosy when the auctioneer reaches the lots of " Sundries " which used to be his own particular perquisite at the sales. As for books he regards them with increasing terror, and pointedly averts his head when the auctioneer puts several lots together and demands a bob. And we notice that he is no longer so free with his pet phrase " It'll come in handy." When he uses it nowadays he adds the uncomfortable proviso: " It may come in handy *if we live long enough*."

For he knows too well that the wheels of chance revolve slowly. Ten long years may pass before the combination of circumstances comes round which makes that old binder, bought for ten shillings, suddenly indispensable to Farmer Dudfield at harvest-time; or which puts into somebody's head the strange notion that one could make the sawn-off top of a Brougham into a summerhouse. Ten long years, or fifteen, or twenty—and who knows that by then the auctioneer with his clerk beside him may not be moving foot by foot along a line of heaped junk neatly laid out in Mr. Higgins's orchard? "What'll you give me for this lot? No offers? Then put the next lot in with it; and the next. There you are. Now who'll say a bob?"

And if so, perhaps to some budding GNL. DLR., a trim ghost in well-cut breeches and bowler-hat, self-important, self-assured, a free ghost in a free country, will whisper: "Go on, Mister. It'll come in handy."

XV

THE BRIGHT NEW combines, two of them crawling in adjacent fields of oats, remind me of painted ships—Phœnician? Greek?—moving through a rippled sea. Wind-tossed, the oats surge against their prows like wavelets, are brushed aside and fall away. Majestically these vessels of the cornfields sail on.

But that was when the sun shone. On a morning of mist the combines were fire-breathing dragons, looming up hugely, roaring and threatening, laying waste all that stood in their path. They are extraordinary things. I suppose they represent one of the most important mechanical inventions of our century; without them the pullulating nations might go hungry. Yet they look old-fashioned. The farmers call them Contraptions, and so they are. The innumerable and complicated bits and pieces which compose them seem to be joined together like a series of afterthoughts. The whole machine would not have looked amiss at the Great Exhibition of 1851; Alfred Lord Tennyson and Queen Victoria might have gazed in awe at it. But to us, accustomed as we are to streamlining, it is clumsy, " okkard-looking ". So of course are the outdated binders okkard-looking, so are mowing-machines and hay-elevators and haysweeps—indeed all farm implements have this angular and awkward air, in which you catch a glimpse of their origins, as you see in a skeleton the pterodactyl behind the bird, the ape as forerunner of the man. It is less true that they were invented than that they evolved; and their ancestry runs back through history to the billhook and the scythe, to the laborious breast plough, the first wooden spade, the first reindeer-scapula with which some tribesman weary of hunting strove to cultivate the earth.

AN UNACCUSTOMED silence possesses the fields when the combines have finished. This sudden hush of September, which all country-men know, is partly due to a falling-off in the volume of the insects' hum; mostly, I think, to the cutting of the corn. Standing corn is in perpetual motion; and as the wind ripples it there is a continual change of light and shade, and of colour too, accompanied by the small ceaseless noise of the shaking-together of the ears. This noise gets louder as the corn ripens. Last week you could hear the oats' murmur from the main road. But today!—

> *Where all day long the wind would trouble*
> *The restless corn on the hill*
> *Lie the shaven fields of stubble*
> *Unfamiliarly still:*
> *Parson's Patch and the Seven Acre,*
> *Folly Furlong and Red Marley,*
> *Where we make for the corncrake*
> *A sanctuary in the tall barley.*
> *Now in vain the accustomed eye*
> *Looks for the sudden catspaws clawing;*
> *Ear misses the oats' sigh*
> *And the landrail's sawing.*
> *All is still where all was motion*
> *And the winds pass silently,*
> *As if we had reaped the ocean,*
> *Harvested the unharvested sea.*

WE SHATTER the silence with our shotguns. *September the First, Partridge shooting begins*, my old pocket diary used to say. (My current one only records *P.A.Y.E. week No. 52 begins*.) But we still walk the biscuit-coloured fields on the first of September.

This was the shooting the Colonel loved: walking-up partridges on hushed mornings when, as he put it, you could almost hear the mushrooms growing. So now at the end of my book let me remember him as I did at the beginning, that green-clad backbent figure beneath the deerstalker. (I believe he possessed only one other hat, a bowler of extraordinary shape, his father's probably, for it was the kind you see in Spy cartoons; the Colonel crammed it down on his grizzled head when he went to the funerals of his friends, which became more frequent as he himself grew older.)

Sweep the famous mole-catcher trots dutifully at his heels as we enter the first stubble-field and walk towards the sun. Late-rising through a white mist it hangs before us like a huge tangerine, and in its light the Colonel's red face burns like virginia creeper upon a south wall. But all the rest of him is green, the hat, the Norfolk jacket, those curious cycling trousers, the rough Harris stockings. He has only to stand still against the background of a hedge, and hey-presto he vanishes!

We walk for a hundred yards before anything happens; then a covey explodes almost beneath my feet, and the air is full of that whickering sound which for as long as I live I shall associate with the feel of the crisp stubble under my boots (rather like the feel of a new toothbrush when you run your finger along it!) and with the little scarlet pimpernel which creeps among the stubble, and with the hot smell of bruised camomile. Bang, bang, all along the line as the chittering covey flies down it; until at the farthest end of the line the banging becomes a mere popping, a toy-gun sound. Puffs of feathers still floating in the quiet air, and the dogs running forward, red setter, golden cocker, liver and white spaniel, Sweep the black Labrador. Tails waving, somebody whistling, somebody calling *seek, seek, seek*. Red setter cantering back, head held high, a fluttering in her jaws; trim little cocker pouncing on something that moves in the stubble; liver and white spaniel puzzled and zigzagging, *seek, seek, seek;* Sweep coming back to the Colonel at a smug trot, the partridge limp in his mouth, feathers in his eyes.

ON FIRSTS of September we would always start punctually at nine and walk until noon, and then it was whisky-time. The Colonel's military precision, his long experience, his habit of thirst, together brought us back to the rickyard at exactly two minutes to twelve; and he led us into the farmhouse through the big kitchen with its flagstoned floor. Here he turned out the contents of his capacious shooting-bag, in which there were sure to be some mushrooms mixed up with the partridges and cartridges and blood and feathers; toadstools too if he had found any, for " a tot of whisky will quell 'em, me boy " should they happen to be poisonous. Unexpected things, as I told you before, were liable to come out of the Colonel's bag: a live slow worm, a dead weasel. He was a kind of kleptomaniac of the fields. Why? He liked, I think, to handle at leisure these live and dead creatures, curiosities, odds and sods, " common objects of the countryside " as the old nature books called them. He saw a sinuous beauty in the slow worm, drew back the weasel's lip to admire its sharp little teeth. " If I were a rabbit now,—*that'd* be what I'd see in a nightmare! " I have watched him stroking, lovingly and half-regretfully, the blue cheek-feathers of a jay he had shot: " Charmin' little birds—pity we have to kill 'em." There was nothing hypocritical about his regrets; but even if the jay had not been ' vermin' he would probably have shot it just the same. He was somewhat trigger-happy, quick on the draw if he saw any unfamiliar bird or beast; he fired at it in order to find out what it was. Once, out partridge-shooting, he bagged a macaw. It belonged to a rich neighbour of his who kept a private zoo. Besides being rich this man was happy-go-lucky and eccentric; his captives often escaped, or perhaps he let them go upon the whim of the moment. The macaw, squawking loudly, flew out of a hedge straight towards the Colonel, who slew it, as he said afterwards, more or less in self-defence;

for he wasn't quite sure whether it came out of a whisky-bottle.

THE SHOOTING-LUNCH at the farmhouse went on for nearly two hours. There was always a ham from one of the Colonel's own pigs, sweet-cured in molasses flavoured with juniper and spices, the most delicious ham I have ever tasted, then there was an enormous apple-pie made with some special kind of apple, known as a Tomkins' Seedling, which nobody but the Colonel had ever heard of but which had a curious winey flavour and a firm flesh that went pinkish when it was cooked. There was also a knobbly cottage loaf, with farmhouse butter and a whole Stilton cheese. The Colonel was an expert on cheese, and he cared for his Stilton lovingly, keeping it at the proper temperature wrapped in a cloth which was damped slightly from time to time; he never, as the barbarians do, spoilt its flavour by pouring into it beer or stout or port. It was one of his pet theories that you could equate civilisation with cheese; and that whether by coincidence or by favour of heaven only those nations were truly civilised that had devoted themselves successfully to the arts of the dairy. Of course the English came out on top, having Stilton, Cheddar, Cheshire, Double Gloucester, Blue Vinny and Wensleydale, but the Colonel allowed that the French and Italians, although foreigners, ran us pretty close with their Camembert and Gorgonzola; the Swiss too, for the sake of Gruyère, though they lost a few marks for selling 'processed' cheeses wrapped in silver paper. But the rest were nowhere. Whoever heard of an American cheese worth eating? Canada's mousetrap was despised even by mice. Australia and New Zealand hadn't grown up; when they had they would perhaps learn to make something half as good as Stilton. The Irish, with some of the best dairyland in the world, were incapable of producing a cheese that wasn't as tasteless as a potato. Barbarians again! As for Germany, that demonstrated her lack of civilisation so violently every generation—have you ever heard tell, demanded the Colonel, of a self-respecting German cheese?

So perhaps his quaint theory had a grain of sense in it. His yardstick for the measurement of civilisation might be an odd one, but at any rate it was not so absurd as the current American standard, which judges a whole people by the modernity of their plumbing.

AFTER LUNCH we would set out again over the stubbles that lay golden in the afternoon sun. We never made a great bag on these occasions, for we walked leisurely and as the Colonel grew old he became more and more inclined to pause in a gateway for a chat and a cigarette. He'd turn out his shooting-bag and demonstrate how one could infallibly tell a young partridge from an old one (" Bend back the upper mandible of its beak to see whether it's soft or hard "). Or he'd admire a " red-legged un " he'd shot, a French partridge which he always called a Froggie. Or he'd ask us about an old song he'd heard, the Twelve Days of Christmas, which has the refrain ' And a partridge in a pear-tree '. Now who the devil, said he, ever saw a partridge sitting in a pear-tree,— or indeed in any sort of tree whatever? " I bet it was a little owl; or maybe it was a missel-thrush puffed-out on a cold day." None of us could explain that line; and to this day I can't make even a guess about the meaning of ' a partridge in a pear-tree '.

When the cigarettes were finished we moved on, across the stubbles that darkened as the sun declined. The brown coveys rose and scattered; the guns banged; the dogs wove to and fro in front of us whenever the line stood still. And when at tea-time we came to the last stubble and drove it in towards the farmhouse the sun was sinking low behind us and our long shadows went before, we were giants. With seven-league boots I seemed to stride down the hill. The Colonel, with his gun over his shoulder, was a Long Man with his club upraised, as we came down the last steep slope to the huddled byres.

BUT all that was long ago. I remember the last time, which was in 1938. I stayed behind after the farmhouse tea, and the Colonel took me round his garden to show me the apricots ripening against the wall. He picked one and ate it and said that one of the little pleasures of life was eating a sun-warmed apricot which you'd grown yourself and picked off the tree. This set us talking about little pleasures, and the Colonel asked me if I realised how much of the fun of living depended upon them. " No, dammit, of course you don't; you're too young. But wait a little while, and you'll see what I mean." As we walked along the garden path he bent down (it hurt him to bend, for he'd stiffened up after the long day's walking) and picked up an acorn. " Look at it, so neat in its little egg-cup—how perfectly it fits—how *pretty* it is—ever since I was a child I've enjoyed staring at an acorn at least once a year! " We talked about the special things which gave us this particular kind of wonder or delight. Chestnuts just out of their spiny shells; hedgesparrows' eggs, said I, transparent blue like the tempera colour of the sky in an Italian Primitive painting; an orange-tip butterfly, said he, sitting on an umbel in the April sun. What about a green hairstreak, said I, wings folded so that the vivid underside shows, on a hawthorn-bush in May? Birdsong, said the Colonel; not the famous singers only, but the blackcap and the sedge-warbler and the jenny wren with her small unassuming song as she pauses for a moment among the hedge-roots? Then we talked of smells. Wet earth after a drought; tomatoes; bruised bracken; the smell of geranium leaves on your hands when you've been taking cuttings; the smell of a weir; stables; the apple-picking smell; a squitch-fire on an autumn evening.

And so we went on. I didn't know then that the Colonel was dying; maybe he didn't know himself, when he added to our catalogue beech-leaves in the spring, and the silvery buds on the wayfaring tree, and a glimpse of foxes teaching their cubs to play, and the affectionate purring noise which a sitting hen makes when her eggs are hatching. Did he have an inkling that he wouldn't see another May? Perhaps; but all seasons were sweet to him, and as we turned into the house, and heard the hum of a neighbour's tractor, working late, he turned to me with his old grin and said

" Autumn ploughing! How quick it comes round! Here we are at the arse-end of the year again! "

So the months revolve like the merry-go-round at the Mop. And for my part all I ask is that as I grow older I shall look forward to each turn of the wheel as eagerly as the Colonel did, each month as new as the horse-chestnut out of its shell, each with its small particular contentments and its special small delights: no season sweeter than another, glad of the first frost and glad of the first cuckoo, the brown autumn welcome as the green spring.

THE END

Kemerton
October, 1955